Dancing at the Edge

Dancing at the Edge

Competence, Culture and Organization

in the 21st Century

Second Edition

Maureen O'Hara
Graham Leicester

Second edition: 2019
Reprinted: 2020, 2021, 2024

Published by:
Triarchy Press
Axminster, UK

www.triarchypress.net

ISBNs:
Print: 978-1-911193-67-8
ePub: 978-1-911193-68-5
pdf: 978-1-911193-69-2

Artwork by Jennifer Williams

**Jennifer Williams is critically acclaimed at making hand-made
books, cut-outs, photographs, illustrations, prints and puppets.
She is a trustee and member of International Futures Forum and
for 31 years directed the Centre for Creative Communities.**

tp

Contents

RESPONSES to *Dancing at the Edge* v

FOREWORD – Edgar H. Schein 1

PREFACE TO THE SECOND EDITION 7

INTRODUCTION: Persons of Tomorrow 11

    The World of Tomorrow 11

    Three Emergencies 12

    Culture and Competence 14

    Beyond the Limitations of 20th-Century Competence 17

    21st-Century Competencies 20

    Recognizing 21st-Century Competencies in Practice 23

    Start Where You Are 28

PART ONE: THE CONTEMPORARY CONTEXT 31

CHAPTER 1: Powerful Times 33

    Powerful Times Foretold 33

    Disturbing the Psychosphere 37

    Culture Matters 41

    Stay Hungry, Stay Foolish, Don't Settle 44

CHAPTER 2: Growing with the Times 49

    Defensive Denial 49

    The Growth Response 52

How We Grow 53

Getting Beyond Defensive Denial 56

CHAPTER 3: Competence in the 21st Century 61

The Full Development of the Human Personality 61

The Neurotic Pursuit of Competence 62

Nudging Ourselves to Competence 66

There Is No Hierarchy of Needs 69

Defining Competence 73

PART TWO: 21ST-CENTURY COMPETENCIES 75

CHAPTER 4: Enabling Conditions for 21st-Century
        Competence 77

Three Literacies: Psychological, Cultural and Epistemic .. 77

Competence in Practice 80

Enabling Conditions 83

CHAPTER 5: Being a Person of Tomorrow 87

Four Pillars of Learning 87

Being 88

Humility 90

Balance 94

Faith in the Future 96

CHAPTER 6: Cultural Leadership and the Person of
        Tomorrow 99

Being Together 99

The Importance of Culture 102

Cultural Literacy 103

Navigating the Cultural Landscape 107

Cultural Leadership 109

Changing Cultures 111

CHAPTER 7: Knowing Like a Person of Tomorrow 115

The Enlightenment and Beyond 115

Containing Multitudes 116

Expanding Our Ways of Knowing 118

Knowing and Feeling 120

Knowledge in Motion 122

Maps and Compasses 124

CHAPTER 8: Organizing Persons of Tomorrow 127

The Setting: Places To Grow 127

The Promise of Adhocracy 128

And Its Dangers 130

The Producer 132

Robust Adhocracy 134

Money at the Margins 138

CHAPTER 9: Persons of Tomorrow in Action 141

Becoming Through Doing..141

What Kind of Action? 144

Messy and Complex 144

Hopeful and Wise 146

Patient and Reflective..148

The Master of Go 149

Theatres for Action Learning..................................151

Rehearsal Spaces 153

CHAPTER 10: Practical Hope 157

    Start Where You Are.. 157

    Inspiration 159

    Prompts.. 161

    Form A Creative Integrity..................................... 162

    Reflect and Learn.. 163

    Never Forget the Bigger Game 165

CHAPTER 11: Conclusion 167

    Why Last Chapters Disappoint 167

    Blowing An Uncertain Trumpet 168

REFERENCES... 171

NOTES 189

INDEX 189

RESPONSES to *Dancing at the Edge*

We want to change the world. But that begins with ourselves. Often our focus is almost incessantly outward with what is wrong out there, without the corresponding reflection upon and assessment of our own skills, attitudes and beliefs. To do such reflection and assessment we need the set of concepts in this book, exquisitely organized around the important concept of 'The Person of Tomorrow'. That person could be you.

Bob Horn, Visiting Scholar in the Human Sciences and Technology Advanced Research Institute (H-STAR) at Stanford University and CEO, MacroVU Inc.

For anyone feeling the challenge of today's world and struggling to find their feet amidst the complexity, this is a book to savour and treasure. Drawing on long experience, wide research and deep reflection the authors build on the simple statement that 'the first step is awareness' to take us on a journey of deepening our inherent capacities to meet the world through transformative growth and learning in action. It is refreshing and valuable to find a book that recognises the importance of bringing our whole complex human capacity to the task of systems transition, renewal and regeneration. We can look for patterns and design pathways. But it is always persons, working together, who make the journey to the third horizon. If we want to shift the culture, we have to do something counter-cultural, we have to dance at the edge. Take this book with you.

Bill Sharpe, author, *Three Horizons: The patterning of hope*

As a set of guidelines to how we should think and act in powerful and liquid times, this is an excellent start, ably assisted by the distinctive artwork of Jennifer Williams that sets a questing tone, and the handsome production values of Triarchy Press.

Michael Marien, Global Foresight Books

Leadership Development is an industry and like all industries it has its own marketing strategies. One is coming up with fancy labels and new ideas rather than considering real need. But does it help organizations solve their challenges to jump on the next bandwagon leadership approach? Or are we in the innovation trap of leadership and people development – not taking care of what is proven and still valuable to apply, to be combined with additional approaches, methods and tools.

The work of Leicester and O'Hara is different. It provides an orientation to the field and is based on solid philosophical and historical thinking. It makes you think and reflect and it is a good starting point for coping with the variety of challenges emerging in today's environment. I like the book because it makes me think and it encourages me to take these ideas as a starting point for all my actions in my professional environment. Especially the idea of transitioning from a socialized mind to a self-transforming mind, which has become the compass/quest for all my thoughts and actions.

The book in three words: inspiring, motivating, enabling.

Peter Spannagl, Global Talent and Inclusion, Bayer

In business today there is a permeating sense that the toolbox of management practices developed over the last 50 years is not enough to equip leaders to navigate these complex times and deliver sustainable results. There is much discussion and literature supporting the need for more transformational leaders, yet very little practical advice on how to develop these abilities. This is where I see the work of Leicester and O'Hara making a profound contribution to the next level of leadership development. Exploration of the Psychological, Cultural and Epistemic literacies provides a blueprint for individuals to grow the competencies needed to face the challenges of today and tomorrow in an adaptive manner. This book gives me hope that through a deeper connection with our innate humanism and having the courage to work at the edge of our abilities we can collectively create a better future for all humanity.

Susan Francis, Leadership Development Consultant

Dancing at the Edge is a comprehensive examination of the times we live in – straddling two paradigms of consciousness, one losing credibility ever more rapidly while a new one is being born but is not yet ready to be embraced by the masses. The authors explore the challenges facing any of us who are trying to midwife this new paradigm, which they call "persons of tomorrow". I love one quote they cite from a Native American woman dealing with the vanishing of the buffalo, which was at the heart of her people's culture: "I am trying to live a life I do not understand." Many people might say something like this today. If you see yourself as a leader of change, read this book!

John Renesch, author, *The Great Growing Up*

For those looking for hope in this increasingly perilous century, this book points helpfully inward to ourselves. It challenges us to see and to be among the sturdy individuals whose balanced wisdom, humility and faith in the future can lead us safely, 'dancing at the edge' of human survival.

Elsa Porter, Fellow of the US National Academy of Public Administration

A life-enhancing exploration of the new work to which we are now called: out-growing modernity by practising the art of becoming self-transcending persons committed to nurturing the emergence of self-transcending cultures. A book to be read, digested and embodied.

Ruben Nelson, Executive Director, Foresight Canada

This is the kind of book that is deceptively thin, since it is so dense with meaning that you need to pause every 3-5 pages to digest what you read. Graham Leicester and Maureen O'Hara have partnered seamlessly to create a mind-expanding book that conveys both a sense of urgency for what our world and societies are experiencing, and a sense of hope for what is possible for each one of us to do. I recommend the book wholeheartedly and encourage you to find out about the work of International Futures Forum and get involved!

Elina Koussis, Leadership Development Learning Leader

Humanity is now clearly at the 'edge of chaos' – a place of danger and potential, where we are given the chance to grow up and unfold our highest potential and creativity to unleash a transformative response. I have been blessed to be nourished by the wisdom circle that is the International Futures Forum for over a decade now. This 2nd edition of the insightful classic **Dancing at the Edge** *could not be released at a more timely moment. Read it, reflect on each chapter, start conversations about it with your neighbour, in your community or at work. From such conversations and the actions that follow we will prove C.G. Jung right: "we don't solve our problems, we outgrow them". Humanity is now invited to step into mature membership of the community of life. Maureen and Graham have created a wonderful provocation that might help us to dance our way out of this mess and actively choose a regenerative future for all.*
Daniel Christian Wahl, author, *Designing Regenerative Cultures*

Maureen and Graham have tuned up the dance steps on how to navigate our way in this complex and fascinating world. Their steps include a wonderfully comprehensive variety of frameworks and ideas, so you can combine set pieces with a bit of improv.

I have bought many copies of the 1st edition and people have found it an enlightening resource on how to be a person of tomorrow, today! Let's expand the dance floor and create a tomorrow that works for each and all. I often read 300-page books and find they could have been a 10-page article. **Dancing at the Edge** *feels like a 150-page book that could easily have been double that length. Kudos to Graham and Maureen for condensing so much wisdom in this wonderful small book.*
Douglas O'Loughlin, PhD, Civil Service College Institute of Leadership and Organisation Development, Singapore

Much has already been said about competence in the age of complexity. This book profoundly reweaves the context of the inquiry on competence with imagination and empathy for how whole persons and whole systems can transform and flourish. Clarity, conciseness and complexity, all inside 200 pages!
Aftab Omer, President, Meridian University

The most thoughtful leaders on the frontlines of philanthropy and impact investing know that the stakes are going up even as "best" practices are not keeping up. This thoughtful book challenges those seeking transformative, systems change to begin close in: by asking ourselves how we must change to meet the world's growing complexity. Many have asked this question, but few have addressed it as generatively and creatively as O'Hara and Leicester. **Dancing at the Edge** *will expand your sense both of what is necessary and what is possible.*

Katherine Fulton, co-founder, Monitor Institute

The first edition of **Dancing at the Edge** *became my guide – it helped me navigate through the uncertainty of our times, it gave me validation for some of the choices I had made and the way I was living, and it helped me find a wider community of other people who were also 'dancing at the edge'. There is a lot of wisdom in this text, as with so much of the International Futures Forum's work. Much of the content in the book is ahead of its time, but I can assure you if you read this now you will be grateful for it for many years to come, and will continue to find it a relevant and reassuring compass.*

Cassie Robinson, Head of Digital Grant Making at The National Lottery Community Fund and Co-founder of the Point People

This extraordinary book offers that most precious commodity: hope. For the policymaker struggling with complexity and mess, we learn that we already have everything we need to take effective action and help create the future. To flourish in powerful times, personal growth is no longer merely an option; it is a necessity. An inspiring, humane and practical guide to activating the competencies latent within us all.

Joe Griffin, Director, Early Learning and Childcare, Scottish Government

FOREWORD – Edgar H. Schein

This book is a remarkable paradox. It is certainly not a 'How-to' book that teaches you some new skill to make you a better leader. Rather, it is a deep dive into what is going on in and around us that we must understand in order to cope with today's and tomorrow's realities. So it is a How-to book that asks nothing less of you than that you become a new person; a book that will enable you to understand and change what is going on and, in that process, will not only make you a better person, but enable you to make a better world. The authors, one a Rogerian clinician and organizational psychologist, the other a former diplomat and policymaker, have a deep understanding of the challenges that face the world and provide in this book a challenge to us as readers to get on board and take this deep dive with them.

This book reviews and analyses the pressing global problems of today from a psychological, social, and most of all cultural perspective, and invites us to think about and engage with this level of complexity. The problems which human society faces on a planet that may not be able to sustain that society much longer are, by definition, complex, multifaceted and systemic. And, inasmuch as we are coping with open, dynamic, and unpredictable events, many of these problems are *unknowable* at this stage. The challenge for humanity, then, is to develop the capacity to deal with potentially difficult challenges *that are not yet known*. What capacities will be required in humans to deal with such unknown problems and to overcome our tendencies to deal with the attendant anxieties by denial, rationalization and passive resignation?

Those anxieties come in two forms: what we have called *survival anxiety* or the recognition we must do something if we are to survive, and *learning anxiety* or the fear we may not be able to learn what we need to do to survive (Schein & Schein, 2019).

1

The paradox of actively managing the learning process is whether it is better to heighten survival anxiety – scare ourselves so much that we finally take some sort of action – or to identify the barriers to learning, to reduce our learning anxiety and get to work on some adaptive learning efforts.

Adaptive learning efforts do not specify the problem that we are trying to solve in very precise terms (such as, for example, reducing the amount of plastic in the ocean), but recognize that from our efforts to do something specific that we can already do, we learn more about the as yet unknown problems that we may face tomorrow.

One of the most profound conclusions these authors reach is that such adaptive learning begins with ourselves, with our own capacity to see beyond our immediate context and grasp through our relationships with others the broader perspective that is needed for this new learning. As the authors point out, our incredible brains give all of us the capacity for this broader learning, but growing up within a given culture with a given language also predetermines what we learn and how we learn, leading to a second paradoxical issue of how to proceed.

If we accept that culture largely determines what we see, how we interpret it, what values and meanings we attach to things, our emotional responses to our experience, and, in the end, our actions, how can we, as fish, not only discover the water that we swim in, but transform that water into something new and better? It would seem that the key to such learning is to expose ourselves to different cultures, and jump into new waters either by travelling and learning new languages or by exploring more deeply the variation in the water of our own fish tank by systematically exploring the subcultures that exist in our own society. Or preferably do both.

These points raise the whole issue of who can best benefit from this deep dive into an uncertain future, this exquisitely detailed analysis of what is really going on. Read this as a traveller, let the many landscapes broaden your thinking rather than leading you to a sudden insight, a moment for understanding, and a call to action. You won't find such clarity, but you will develop a much broader perspective which will enable you to see more clearly and enable you to evolve more alternatives for your own action.

It is tempting to go to the usual prescription that this book is of special importance for leaders. In our culture we have been taught that power and information, and therefore the capacity to act, sits at the top of the organization, and we have been taught that people who sit at the top of organizations should be thought of as leaders and should, therefore, be the initiators of the kind of adaptive changes we need. The reality in most organizations is that the heads are more caretakers, administrators, and managers.

If we define *leadership* as *creating something new and better*, then we discover that leadership can, does, and should occur all through the organization, and that the most important thing for people at the top to do is to create a climate and a context for personal growth to flourish at all levels, to make it possible for everyone in the organization and in society more broadly to begin their personal learning journey to discover something new and better. In order to create something new and better, *we all must learn* to become more conscious of ourselves, of our relationships, how we work in groups, and how our existing culture controls our lives. Our formal leaders should help us do this.

Paradoxically what we see in Western culture, particularly in the US culture which is fundamentally built around rugged individualism and competition, is people in positions of power actually creating the conditions that *undermine learning* by creating work climates that make it unsafe for people to speak truth to power, to take time out for reflection, and to improve the immediate world they live in.

We find in many of our organizations that maintaining distant professional relationships, staying in one's role, is the cultural ideal, even as we find that individualistic competition creates toxic relationships and pathological group processes. To break out of this mindset will require personal learning throughout society, otherwise the culture will not evolve to deal with the unexpected learning challenges that we face.

3

The good news is that as humans we all have the capacities and competencies that this book lays out as being necessary for gradual cultural evolution to occur. The other good news, based on my experience of observing various kinds of managers and leaders for over 60 years, is that we have seen such learning leaders throughout history creating new kinds of organization, new political processes, and new values around which to build relationships.

We see such learning leaders in all kinds of organizations today, especially in the arts and other non-profit organizations, but many of them have to constantly fight the cultural forces that encourage regression to the safety of individualistic, competitive hierarchy. In all such cases the individual insights that enabled them to do something new and better came from cross-cultural experiences that allowed them to see and analyse the water they were swimming in as captive fishes. We labelled this "Humble leadership: the power of relationships, openness and trust" (Schein & Schein, 2018) and argued, as this book does, that the winds of change are blowing more strongly than ever within young organizations and with the new generations that bring new values and perspectives to work.

In every sense this book is a wake-up call to all of us to begin our personal learning journeys to broaden our perspective, to build more collaborative relationships, to get used to the new learning processes that will have to develop. When I taught a course at MIT called "Managing planned change", I asked all students to make a *personal change* by the end of the semester, and in various project groups to make a *change in their university and urban environment*. To my amazement, all the individuals and all the groups were successful in making changes, but perhaps the most significant learning for all of us was discovering how the interplay between the personal change issues and the group process change issues educated each other. We discovered how our own personal resistance to change usefully informed and provided empathy for the people whom we were trying to change in our group project.

So my advice to readers of this book is to begin with both some intention to enlarge your own perspective through travelling, reading, becoming observant and reflective, and start experimenting a bit with making your relationships more personal and illuminating. The level of culture change that will be required to save the planet and us in it will, in the end, depend on each of us starting such learning processes.

Edgar H. Schein
Sloan Fellows Professor of Management Emeritus
MIT Sloan School of Management

PREFACE to the Second Edition

This is the second edition of a book we first published in 2012. For the most part it is a judicious revision rather than a wholesale rewrite – although there is substantial new content including one new chapter.

There are good reasons for the update. First and most important is the success of the first edition. The book has found an audience, hit its mark. As Ed Schein says in his thoughtful and generous new Foreword, this is a "deep dive into what is going on in us and around us that we must understand in order to cope with today's and tomorrow's realities". It is also a book full of hope: that we have within us the competencies and capacities we need to take on the challenges we face – if we can find the supportive settings in which to discover and develop them.

That leads to the second reason. Since the first edition was published the 'powerful times' we described as the 21st-century operating environment have shown no sign of abating. We have brought some of the early contextual material up to date with more contemporary references. We also offer some reflections on having identified President Barack Obama in 2012 as a 'person of tomorrow' displaying 21st-century competence at the highest level, given what has transpired since. But the thrust of the narrative was sound in the first edition and remains essentially unchanged even if the stakes now seem higher.

As the challenges became more apparent, we had the great good fortune to work with our friend and colleague Alex Grimshaw at PPS International, a boutique leadership development consultancy, on the response. Together we have translated the original book into workshop and experiential learning materials which we have used for a variety of corporate, government, community, NGO and non-profit programmes to develop the 21st-century competencies in practice and in a professional context.

This experience, working with a rich diversity of programme participants from different cultures and different demographics, has inevitably enhanced our own learning and fuelled further exploration. Through the process we have been able to tighten up the conceptual architecture that underpins the book as we have found it resonating with people's experience and as we ourselves have thereby gained more confidence in it. We hope the book, in its early chapters, now expresses these foundations more clearly.

We were struck by a comment from one early workshop participant who observed simply that 'The first step is awareness'. That has stayed with us. It is right that in order to develop our 21st-century competencies we first need to become more adept at reading the landscape we are operating in and our own individual and collective responses to it. What we seek to bring to awareness can be articulated in three sets of three: three emergencies, three responses and three literacies.

We now explicitly invite readers to consider three interrelated but distinct 'emergencies' as characteristic of the times: a real emergency – the challenges we face in the world; a conceptual emergency – the struggle to make sense of the complexity well enough to address these challenges; and an existential emergency – how all of this leaves us feeling at a human level, individually and collectively.

We note that a typical human response to overwhelm and confusion, both individually and collectively, is defensive denial ('it's not happening'), a stance that takes considerable effort and energy to maintain and therefore can dissipate into chaotic collapse ('I give up'). But there is a third, creative response – growth and transformation – in which we acknowledge the messiness and confusion and choose to learn our way through it.

That learning is in turn enabled by the awakening and development of three capacities we need to read this landscape, three literacies – psychological literacy, cultural literacy and epistemic literacy. The 'map' that this structure of three emergencies, three responses and three literacies provides has proven robust and useful over the years and so is reinforced in the first part of the book.

Finally, we have added a new chapter – Chapter 10 – on 'practical hope'. If the first step is awareness, the second step is practice. We stress throughout that competence can only be expressed and demonstrated in action. As the challenges we face in the world become more urgent, so the demand for effective and responsible action has only grown in the years since first publication. It has been a feature of our development programmes, for example, in which participants have been eager to design and deliver their own 'small acts of creative transgression' both to express their 21st-century competencies and to help shift their professional culture in the direction of something more conducive to their development. The promise of 21st-century competence is the rediscovery of agency in the face of a confusing and unknown future, in which we cannot simply follow precedent but must brave uncertainty. There is no roadmap, only a supported process of action learning.

At the same time the wider network of which we are both a part, International Futures Forum, has also found itself pressed towards action. We have been able to collaborate with colleagues to codify the practice of 'transformative innovation' and to make available the tools, frameworks, processes and other resources needed to support it through our online IFF Academy. We are pleased to include reference to these materials in the concluding chapters, confident that many more will now be encouraged to follow the simple suggestion to 'start where you are'.

Maureen O'Hara
Graham Leicester

INTRODUCTION:

Persons of Tomorrow

Turning and turning in the widening gyre
The falcon cannot hear the falconer;
Things fall apart; the centre cannot hold.
           The Second Coming – W B Yeats (1920)

Hold tight, hold tight, we must insist that the
world is what we have always taken it to be.
           The Family Reunion – T S Eliot (1939)

We do not solve our problems, we outgrow them.
           Collected Works – C G Jung (1938)

The World of Tomorrow

In his famous essay, *The World of Tomorrow and the Person of Tomorrow*, first published in 1969 and later expanded, the psychologist Carl Rogers, an American who had worked with groups all over the world, surveyed a rapidly changing landscape at home and abroad and contemplated humanity's future.

As the upheavals of the 1960s played out around him in diverse ways and diverse settings – the beginnings of environmental awareness, social movements advocating equality of gender and race, protests against the seemingly endless war in South East Asia, experiments in communal households, cooperative economies and a revolution in popular culture – Rogers was not the only one to sense a dramatic shift and the struggling emergence of a new world. Theodore Roszak (1969),

11

writing at the same time, captured the spirit of the age in a phrase that has endured: "the making of a counter culture".

While others at the time feared this loosening of cultural constraints and actively worked to suppress the freedom and confusion that ensued, Rogers chose to see this as a creative moment, a moment of growth and possibility. He heard people reaching for new ways to respond to the challenges of the times that were not merely new applications of old solutions but were calling forth new ways of being. What, he wondered, would the world of tomorrow look like? What kinds of challenges would it pose to humanity? What kinds of capacities would the crises and opportunities of the future require of us and help us to develop? What, in other words, might we expect of 'persons of tomorrow'?

"I have an uneasy feeling about this chapter", he wrote. "In some vague way I believe that what I am saying here will some day be fleshed out much more fully, either by me or someone else."

He was right. This book is our attempt to explore, examine and provide our best answers to the critical questions Rogers was asking. Because the challenges, the turbulence and the sense of a world turned upside down that he envisaged have indeed come to pass. Rogers' world of tomorrow is our today.

It is a confusing, complex, fast-changing and radically interconnected place. The forces of suppression and denial are as active as they were in Rogers' day, but now play out against a backdrop narrative of economic, existential, social and even planetary threats. We live in powerful times. There is a pervasive sense of incoherence. The old rules, it seems, no longer apply, however much we cling to them and yearn for the return to a settled past. The new rules have yet to stabilize: everything is in beta, temporary, provisional, waiting for the next upgrade.

Three Emergencies

We have found it helpful in getting to grips with these circumstances to frame humanity's predicament in terms of three 'emergencies' – emergent trends that are gathering pace and threaten to overwhelm us.

There is a *real emergency* (or a 'manifest' emergency – they are all real): the incipient breakdown of systems we used to take for granted, from democratic governance and decision-making to ecological balance, the persistence of poverty and inequality, the challenge of maintaining basic services like healthcare or clean water, the need to shift away from fossil fuels as 'climate change' is increasingly recognised as 'climate emergency'. The list is familiar, daunting and almost without end.

At the same time there is a *conceptual emergency*: the pervading sense of cognitive dissonance experienced when the core concepts we have relied on to make sense of our world are no longer up to the task.[1] Scientific claims are challenged at the highest levels. Plausibility is as powerful as truth. We see what we believe rather than believe what we see – and even then struggle to make sense of the big picture beyond the fragments.

Don Michael (2010) talked about information overload in the world of 'the missing elephant' – in which there is little chance any of us will ever know more than one small piece of the elephant, and there are now so many different pieces, they change so rapidly and they are all so intimately related one to another, that even if we had the technology to put them all together we would still not be able to make sense of the whole. Nor, we might now add, would we believe the results of such an exercise when we can no longer safely distinguish 'fact' from 'deep fake' manipulated reality.

The real and the conceptual emergencies are then felt in what we might term an *existential emergency* in which their effects show up at the level of the human being, individually and collectively. This is what happens when the shared narratives and patterns of life which provide the 'glue' that holds communities and societies together start coming apart. Societies become incoherent and fragmented, we experience 'culture wars', a loosening of cultural solidarity and a loss of faith in shared institutions.

These interpenetrated disruptions strike at the heart of our frameworks for reality. What does it mean to be a person in this world? What am I worth? What anchors my identity, my morality, my sense of purpose, my understanding of what we owe each other? Our collective sanity and sense of continuing existence as a species on a liveable planet is cast into doubt.

The good news is that we can adapt to these new circumstances, we can learn and grow into them. Every culture produces its own form of personhood adapted to life and circumstances in that society. When cultures change personhood changes – just consider the differences in what people find offensive, outrageous or appealing depending on where they were raised.

Already we see new kinds of persons emerging who are more at home in the new complexity and have greater capacity to be effective in the face of the emergencies we describe. Here we ask how this new kind of person – the person of tomorrow – already in our midst and in ourselves may now be encouraged, supported and developed?

There will certainly be technological and intellectual breakthroughs in the coming years to point the way and aid us out of our present predicament. We still need and value the astonishing technical competencies that came to dominate the 20th century. But in any scenario it will continue to fall to people, to human beings, to turn insight into action and to work within existing entrenched systems to shift them in a more hopeful direction. We will need to pay a lot more attention to the additional personal competencies that shift will require. Rogers' thirty-year-old question has assumed a new urgency. How can we develop persons of tomorrow, expressing 21st-century competencies?

Culture and Competence

The first part of this book examines the contemporary context in which we must make good on the potential that Rogers saw in persons of tomorrow. That includes the nature of the challenges we face, but also the pattern of cultural assumptions we make about competence and personal development generally. Because they now lie so deep in the culture, these assumptions can often go unseen.

They too must be re-examined. Competence is culturally determined. What works in one culture fails in another. Cultures and cultural stories provide templates for what it is to be successful in a particular society, to be accomplished, to live a successful life. Rogers was right to see the competencies of persons of tomorrow coming to prominence in parallel with the emergence of a 'world of tomorrow'.

We will find it difficult to discover and nurture 21st-century competencies if we remain in thrall to the cultural story about competence that dominates today. That story suggests, among other things, that competence:

- is a 'thing', a quality of the individual
- can be taught or trained to different levels by following an appropriate curriculum
- can be tested, measured and graded in the abstract
- will ultimately win an economic return both for the competent individual and his or her organization or nation

This used to be a predominantly Western story. But, carried by powerful institutions and incentives – not to mention the meta-system of global capitalism – it has now become prevalent across the globe.

It has certainly enabled a mastery of specialist competencies to date that has been hugely impressive and is to be admired. But it has become all but impossible within this context to recognize or develop the additional 21st-century competencies we now need to thrive in the world we have created.

Three shifts in the culture are therefore critical in our view. The first is to recognize, as the OECD did in a five-year study of "key competencies for the 21st century", that today we must understand competence not as abstract achievement but as "the ability to meet important challenges in life in a complex world".[2]

We endorse that definition. It follows that 21st-century competencies cannot be measured or assessed in the abstract. You can only see them as a whole and in action. They can be demonstrated in, and inferred from, successful performance in complex situations in the real world. They cannot be tested and graded by questionnaires, assessment surveys or written examinations.

The second shift is equally fundamental. In the operating conditions of the 21st century it is impossible to be competent alone. Competence is a function of culture, which is a function of relationship. This is not only a plea for attention to teamwork, collaboration and other competencies relating to an individual's performance in group settings. It is a deeper acknowledgment that we create our own lives in a pattern of relationship with other lives, and always have done.[3]

Technical competence can be mastered alone. But its application requires engaging within complex webs of connection and relationship – the context of human systems and cultures within which that competence needs to be exercised. The growing interest in qualities like empathy, compassion and emotional intelligence even for the acquisition of technical skills speaks to this dawning recognition in today's hyper-connected world. 21st-century competencies cannot be observed or exercised except in relationship with other people.

Third, 21st-century competencies are qualities of persons as a whole. Becoming a person of tomorrow is not like assembling the parts of a machine. It is difficult to be compassionate, for example, without at the same time showing a capacity for empathy, humility and other qualities. 21st-century competencies must be appreciated holistically. Their expression will fly in the face of a dominant culture that suggests competencies can be distinguished one from another, developed in isolation, and mastered one stage at a time.

We suggest instead that these competencies are innate human capacities and are present in any human system (individual or collective): they simply require the right enabling conditions, settings, life experiences and imagination to be called forth and developed through practice.

In other words, we understand persons of tomorrow as having certain observable inherent attributes and qualities which might then be expressed in practice as identifiable competence – always in the sense of 'the ability to meet important challenges in life in a complex world'. By analogy, a person may have the personal quality or capacity of innate musicality. If that personal quality is matched with the enabling conditions to call it forth in practice (an instrument, a mentor, some people to play with, etc.) then a competence can be developed, which can over time advance to the state of mastery.

In Chapter 3 we explore the late 20th-century culture of the neurotic pursuit of competence. In its place we come down firmly in favour of an earlier expression in the Universal Declaration of Human Rights of 1948: "the full development of the human personality". We reject (as Maslow himself did) the notion of a 'hierarchy of needs': one does not have to achieve shelter in order to graduate to a capacity for love, which can flower and manifest even in the direst of circumstances. So it is with the 21st-century competencies: they are already part of our rich human repertoire of responses, but undervalued, underestimated and so underdeveloped in our late modern culture.

Beyond the Limitations of 20th-Century Competence

It is common in today's polarized culture to make the case for the new by demonizing the old. That is not our intention here. None of this book is intended to decry the value of what we might call '20th-century competencies'. The advances we have made and the structures of education, socialization, professional training and accreditation we have put in place to replicate them at scale have been spectacular. We are not suggesting that the 21st-century surgeon, for example, or any other professional, manager or specialist, can dispense with a thorough technical grounding.

What we are saying is that such competencies, though necessary, are no longer sufficient. We are now in a different world, a VUCA world of cascading crises where every decision is made against a background of volatility, uncertainty, complexity and ambiguity. Once we move from situations that are complicated – such as nuclear engineering – to those that are complex – such as coping with the aftermath of the tsunami that hit the Fukushima nuclear plant in Japan – an entirely other level of competence is required.

We applaud the impact of Atul Gawande's *The Checklist Manifesto: How to get things right* (2009) in reducing error in complex technical processes: it certainly helps to prevent removing the wrong limb in an operating theatre. But as Gawande himself was to discover when his own father was terminally ill, checklists have limits and in some situations might actually reduce competence. The healthcare professional about to engage in a grown-up conversation with a patient about whether to intervene or not towards the end of life needs something more than a tried and tested algorithm to run through. Gawande's later book, *Being Mortal: illness, medicine and what matters in the end*, is not a repudiation of his earlier manifesto but a plea for us to recover our humanity as the context for deploying our technical expertise.

Simply extrapolating our 20th-century competence, and the culture that honours it, into these more complex areas is unlikely to be effective, may be actively counter-productive, and closes off the opportunity to develop the 21st-century competencies we all already possess (to some degree).

Complex problems involving other human beings have no simple answers. They call for a different order of judgement, experience, empathy, personal investment, even wisdom – the capacities of whole persons.

Whilst we have explored the numerous analyses, reports and lists of 21st-century skills, knowledge, competencies, capacities and attributes compiled by others readily available in the business section of any bookstore or in the myriad reports offered by experts in the skills revolution, next generation agile leadership, the future of work and so on, we have chosen to privilege in our own work the observation of people displaying 21st-century competence in practice.

We have found that people who are thriving in the contemporary world, who give us the sense of having it all together and being able to act effectively and with good spirit in challenging circumstances, have some identifiable characteristics in common, even though they are all manifestly themselves – unique and original. They are the people already among us who inhabit the complex and messy problems of the 21st century in a more expansive way than their colleagues.

They do not reduce such problems to the scale of the tools available to them, nor hide behind those tools when they know they are partial and inadequate. They are less concerned with 'doing the right thing' according to standard procedure than they are with really doing the right thing in the moment, in specific cases, with the individuals involved at the time. In a disciplined yet engaging way they are always pushing boundaries, including their own. They dance at the edge.

It is a risky position to take in today's culture. But there is always a sneaking admiration for such people from their more conventional colleagues. These people seem to find it easy – natural in fact – to take a larger, broader, more holistic, more generous, more all-encompassing, altogether bigger view of any circumstance. They have enough identity and value security to be flexible in their actions and responses to encounters with the world while maintaining a reliable ethical stance. They relate to other people in ways that welcome and honour the dignity and possibilities of otherness. They chafe against short-term fixes and 'good enough' responses. They energize others with their vision, their aspiration and their hope.

What is it about such people that enables them to be this way in the face of today's challenges? We do not believe the qualities they display are exceptional. They are innate human capacities that we all possess but which some have managed to develop and express better than others.

Sadly most of us have been brought up and taught to be 'competent' in a dominant culture that has neither appreciated, encouraged nor valued their expression. But for others, the setting they have found themselves in, or the developmental path of their life experience, has put them in circumstances where these 21st-century competencies have been evoked. Some have undertaken dedicated training to enhance their natural capacity.

21st-Century Competencies

The second part of this book elaborates on the qualities, capacities, characteristics and competencies we observe in persons of tomorrow. We will still need to master the technical competencies of the 20th century. But in order to put those competencies to use, to use them wisely and to develop their further potential, we will also need to extend our range.

We take as an organizing framework the four pillars of learning in Jacques Delors' (1996) UNESCO report on education for the 21st century, *Learning: The treasure within*. They are:

- learning to be
- learning to be together
- learning to know
- learning to do

The later chapters in this book explore these four dimensions of 21st-century learning. They describe the qualities of *being* displayed by persons of tomorrow, clustered under the themes of humility, balance and faith in the future. They investigate the essential capacities needed to operate in, and to facilitate, dynamic group situations and work with a high degree of cultural awareness – *being together*. There is a chapter on ways of *knowing* embraced by persons of tomorrow: how to expand our capacity to make sense of a complex and dynamic world whilst simultaneously acknowledging its enduring wonder and mystery.

The final chapters turn to action: *learning to do*. They explore both the new organizational forms that persons of tomorrow are shaping and being shaped by, and the kinds of action learning – wise initiative – that will help to develop the 21st-century competencies in practice, and how to create an enabling environment for their expression in any organization or other work setting. Start where you are.

Underpinning all of these suggestions is the recognition that the first step is awareness. In order to bring our 21st-century competencies to bear on a situation we must both become aware that we possess them and can rely on them and at the same time be able to read the landscape with subtle distinction such that we know when and how to deploy them.

In Chapter 4 we identify three critical 'literacies': ways of seeing, sensing, feeling, knowing, appreciating, 'reading' and making sense of our selves and our circumstances.

The most important is *psychological literacy*. This is a threshold competence: without it the awakening and development of the other 21st-century competencies is very difficult, if not impossible. Essentially it involves a capacity to read and own one's psychological response to challenge and to become master of that response rather than its victim.

Challenge, threat, overwhelm and confusion are frequent operating conditions in today's world and the default psychological defence in these circumstances is denial. It is an automatic response, protective of the psyche and its need for coherence and stability. It requires effort and energy to maintain such defences. When that effort becomes too much we can be swamped by reality and suffer collapse. Denial will protect us for a time, in other words, but it is not a learning stance. Unless we can consciously move beyond it, the deeper resources we all possess are never called into play.

Hence the fundamental importance of the so-called 'double task': to be able to act and reflect on one's actions *at the same time*. When we can recognize our instinctive tendencies towards denial in the face of overwhelm and consciously respond not by avoidance but by trying on other psychological responses for size, we call this 'psychological literacy'.

Epistemic literacy (or knowledge literacy if you prefer) is another kind of awareness – essential in a world beset by conceptual emergency. It refers to the ability to read patterns and assumptions about knowing in the landscape. What counts as valid knowledge in this place at this time? What can I claim to 'know' and how do I know it? What is the pattern of assumptions that underlies my own truth systems, unexamined but now open to inquiry? With epistemic literacy we can move from being trapped in a single, unexamined worldview to an openness to multiple ways of knowing.

Finally, *cultural literacy* involves the capacity to read the culture and the dynamics of systems and groups. We in the West are inadequate – perhaps woefully so – when it comes to understanding the relationship between cultural context and expressions of human qualities. The dominant culture today is hardly conducive to, and in many cases actively resists, the range of qualities and capacities outlined in the pages that follow. These capacities emerge within a culture of their own – more open, receptive, enabling.

If we wish to operate effectively at the level of *cultural* change, we must first be able to see the culture we are in. This is another version of the double task – to be able to act and reflect on the cultural implications of one's actions at the same time. Persons of tomorrow and the culture of tomorrow will grow in parallel, through what our colleague Aftab Omer has referred to as 'cultural leadership'.

The demonstration and development of the 21st-century competencies in many settings will be seen as counter-cultural. Like the football player who stops to tend an injured colleague while the opposition play on and score. Or the teacher who encourages his pupils to ask better questions rather than parrot the required answers. Or the politician who asks her officials to organize a learning journey for her to get a better feel for a messy situation rather than give her a set of statistics to silence the opposition. These are all small acts of cultural leadership, eroding the dominant culture and demonstrating the possibility of working from different assumptions.

These examples are calculated to be low-risk and personal: individuals committing small acts of creative transgression against the norm, choosing in those moments to privilege other values than those typically favoured by the dominant culture. But it is only a matter of degree that separates these acts from more intentional cultural leadership, interventions deliberately taken – in public – to shift the culture (Omer, 2005).[4]

It is a dangerous role. Established cultures fight back. Breaking rules, especially unwritten ones, creates tension at the boundary between the actual and the possible. Admittedly, it takes courage. It is a particular tragedy to see so little willingness to stretch those boundaries in the realm of political leadership. There we find some exceptional figures like Nelson Mandela, Vaclav Havel and Aung San Suu Kyi, ready to stand for a more expansive culture and lead a people towards their vision.[5] They outflank their opponents by playing a bigger game, one that resonates with our better selves. But for the most part those we place in positions of political leadership neglect the potential to use that platform for cultural leadership. They insist on playing the game at a lower level of development and aspiration, reinforcing a dominant culture that keeps our higher potentials in check.

Even if not cut out for cultural leadership on the national scale, at the very least the person of tomorrow must have a high degree of cultural literacy: an ability to read and sense a culture, or a group, and to understand how far it might be willing to move. That literacy may help to identify a suitable existing culture in which to grow. Or it will help to develop such a culture through thoughtful, considered acts of creative transgression. And if practised at a large enough scale or for high enough stakes, it will catalyse the evolution of the culture as a whole.

Recognizing 21st-Century Competencies in Practice

For many years now we have been aware that the modern world

is both driving us crazy (literally: there is a global epidemic of mental illness and mental distress[6]), and that it is throwing up challenges that we are struggling to address with our current levels of competence. Much of our practical work during these years, principally as part of the International Futures Forum (IFF), has been in supporting people to take on complex, messy, seemingly intractable problems – in health, education, community development, governance, enterprise, the arts – wherever they show up. That work has allowed us to observe at first hand the competencies that make a difference in today's world and ways in which they can be encouraged and developed. The competencies explored in the second part of this book are in part derived from that extensive practice.

At the same time we have also been looking for people more at home and more effective in the "blooming, buzzing confusion" of the 21st century: persons of tomorrow expressing 21st-century competencies.

Expecting to find these capacities in today's successful leaders, we have actively shadowed a number of chief executives in different sectors to discover both the secrets of their mastery and how they came by them. The results are reported in Chapter 4. These encounters helped us realize that our established leaders are just as likely to be operating 'in over their heads' as everyone else.

However, we did learn that some settings are more conducive to the demonstration of 21st-century competencies than others. Leader and organizational setting develop together, each level mutually enabling the other. That too is counter-cultural for a leadership development industry that thrives on specialist programmes, awaydays, retreats and other processes based on the unspoken assumption that it is the leader who shapes the organization and that improving the competencies of the former will inevitably impact the latter. We found repeatedly that, in today's contexts, leadership is a relational, emergent process where the actions of followers enable the capacities of leaders, and leaders do best when they attune to the deeper aspirations of their followers.

We also saw some highly impressive individuals in action. And we began to realize that we had seen the 21st-century qualities they displayed in others we have worked with who operate in roles below the chief executive level in their organizations: headteachers, public service directors, nursing managers, middle-ranking officials and countless others. These are people with enough authority in their roles to try something different, but not so much as to be afraid to do so.

It has been tempting to offer more prominent and well-known examples. The truth is they are few and far between. And high-profile cultural leaders will inevitably be viewed with ambivalence as they seek to play out on a public stage the impossible balancing act of being hospice worker for the dying culture and midwife for the new. They cannot help but disappoint one side or the other some of the time. That has always been true, but in an incoherent age which sends people scurrying to the poles for security rather than the centre, even more so – especially in politics.

Even so, while we were writing the first edition of this book the person who exemplified for us the essential aspects of 21st-century competence, playing out before us the ups and downs, the struggles and the paradoxes, of being a person of tomorrow in today's world, was then US President, Barack Obama.

We considered using another example for this new edition. New Zealand Prime Minster Jacinda Ardern was widely praised, for example, for her humanity, compassion and moral strength in her response to an attack by a lone gunman on a mosque in Christchurch in 2019 which resulted in the death of 51 people. The attack, incidentally, was live-streamed on social media by the perpetrator, another feature of an age in which old boundaries are dissolving.

In the end we concluded we still have much to learn from the example of Obama. We are becoming more attuned to discerning 21st-century competence on the world stage, perhaps in view of other models of political leadership now more prominently on display both in the US and elsewhere. Obama continues to offer a study in how those competencies might show up in the political arena and also, since he continues to perform his role as a cultural leader even out of office, a barometer for their wider appreciation. If only to root the concepts we outline in this book in some kind of shared experience, therefore, we continue to reference Obama as an example of what we are talking about.

This is a risk on two levels. First, it may put off half our readers. But believe us when we say we are not making a political point, simply seeking to bring to life by reference to a common source some of the capacities we describe.

Second, like so many before him, Obama may yet fall from grace. If he is anything like the rest of us, he surely has feet of clay – and these will be exposed at some point, apparently making laughable any claim to 21st-century capacities.

That is the fatal flaw in many books of this type – like the companies in Jim Collins's *Good to Great* that became not so great after publication.[7] But in the end, as our own small act of cultural leadership, we believe we must recognize 21st-century competencies where they show up, especially in such a public figure as Obama.

We notice, for example, that his would-be successors amongst the Democrats continue to embrace and appreciate Obama, the qualities of the man, even if they distance themselves from 'Obama-ism' the programme (Linskey, 2019). We note that he left office with good grace and has schooled his supporters to follow his example in service of a more tolerant culture. In November 2016, for example, at a campaign rally in North Carolina for Hillary Clinton shortly before the election, he was heckled by an elderly gentleman. The crowd started booing, shouting the heckler down. It was small stuff compared with what had been happening at Republican rallies in the same campaign. But Obama stopped them in their tracks. "Hold up!" he said. "Hold up!" Then when they eventually quietened: "First of all, we live in a country that respects free speech. Second of all, it looks like maybe he might have served in our military and we gotta respect that. Third of all, he was elderly and we gotta respect our elders. And fourth of all, don't boo. Vote." It was an object lesson, delivered instinctively in the moment, in the practice of tolerance and the requirements for a mature democratic culture.

There are many memorable examples of such cultural leadership to draw on in Obama's case and there are likely to be more in the future. Think back, for example, to January 2011 and the shooting of Congresswoman Gabrielle Giffords at a 'meet the people' event in a supermarket car park in Tucson. The attack, in which six people died and Giffords was seriously injured, shocked America. Some saw it as the inevitable outcome of a politics become intolerant and 'uncivil'. The Republican politician Sarah Palin, then widely seen as contemplating a Presidential bid herself, was vilified for having shown Giffords caught in the crosshairs of a rifle sight as a campaign 'target'. She attempted to address the damage with a speech mourning the dead, but vigorously defending free speech and forthright debate as key American virtues.

It fell to Obama in his public role to address the memorial service for the dead. With the eyes of the world and of a shattered local community watching, how would he respond? It was a test of competence at a high level, way beyond politics. Visibly emotional, yet steadfast, he addressed the service as a cultural leader. He ministered to a cultural wound. He remembered the dead – personally, individually, as if they had each been his neighbour. He praised those who had acted swiftly and selflessly to limit the slaughter – moving the audience to whooping like a campaign rally.

And he used the occasion, this opening in the culture, to call on everyone to reflect on how we live our own lives: to "expand our moral imaginations", "sharpen our instincts for empathy" and remember that "what matters is not wealth, or status, or power, or fame – but rather, how well we have loved".

It is a simple message. Not original by any means. Palin had played with some of the same sentiment. But her intent was clearly political. Obama was operating at another level and calling on our better selves to join him there. It was evocative – a conscious rising to the occasion, calling forth resources already present in the hearts of his audience by authentically demonstrating them himself.

This is setting the bar high. But we can see in this performance some of the common characteristics we have observed in many others in more humdrum, less public, settings. There is a cultural fluency evident in Obama's playing back and forth across domains of family, preacher and politician, local friend and national leader. That is perhaps associated in his case with being – like so many 21st-century persons – the product of a hybrid culture himself. We see an emotional maturity, a lack of fear in dealing with powerful emotions and naming them in public. And a humility in his identification with everyman that would sound false in many others.

This public address was a masterclass in 21st-century competencies, and even today widely recognized as such. As one of the hard-bitten CBS news commentators who was present put it: "I was sitting there and I realized, 'This guy might be a great man'. I had forgotten about that."

Start Where You Are

We wrote this book to share our learning from many years' observing and working with persons of tomorrow, admiring their competence and facility and wondering how to help make a large enough dent in the culture to allow more such practice to flourish. We hope our writing it, and more particularly your reading it, will help to progress that goal.

Since publishing the first edition there have been many more opportunities to learn about the 21st-century competencies in action. We are inspired by the multitude of projects under way that are changing the concrete conditions of life for many people around the world and which, pursued through participation in a variety of new ways of organizing and collaborating, are also enabling those involved to grow into new ways of being. People getting together to "meet important challenges in life in a complex world" (as the OECD definition has it) are providing the spaces and places and opportunities for a fuller range of human capacities to emerge.

Books are only part of the process of change. The truth is that our culture will shift and the 21st-century competencies will be developed only through practice. You cannot learn to play the cello by reading a book, although gaining a technical understanding will provide a sound foundation. And whilst books of advice can help, you will not get fit unless you go through the process of exercise. The 21st-century competencies are like that. The real challenge for all of us is first to raise our awareness of the circumstances we find ourselves in and then to develop our capacity as persons of tomorrow wherever we are, working with whomever we are working with, in whatever setting we find ourselves in today.

Naturally there are places, programmes, support networks, specific courses and the like that may well have a role to play, including those we have developed based on this book since its first publication. That is like going to the gym and taking on a personal trainer. Better still if you can incorporate this 'exercise' into your normal day-to-day working life. In the end, individual and setting must evolve and develop together. It is a harder road, but we believe ultimately more fulfilling and more impactful, if we are able to bring our 21st-century selves to work and to our communities and grow a new culture around us whilst we are there.

The qualities and competencies outlined in this book should give us all we need to do that. We all have it in us to become persons of tomorrow, to rise above denial, and to take on the challenges of today's powerful times.

PART ONE:

THE CONTEMPORARY CONTEXT

CHAPTER 1:

Powerful Times

Powerful Times Foretold

We live in powerful times.[8] For several decades now a growing chorus of commentators, researchers, visionaries of the future and acute observers of the present have been tracking the story of a world changing so fast and so fundamentally that it is spiralling beyond our capacity to understand or control.

The narrative of crisis, upheaval and threatened collapse is now well honed, with observers of governance, economics and environmental sustainability painting a vivid and often bleak picture of a world full of surprises, questioning our competence to deal with the fast-moving realities we face.

This has been coming for some time. By the early decades of the 20th century the realization that modernity had unexpected side effects in the form of massive destabilization was already clear. Phillip Blom (2008) marks the great Paris exhibition of 1900 as the start of what he calls 'the vertigo years' – an unsettling time for the 'nervous generation' living through the great changes leading up to the First World War. Empires were crumbling. The 600-year-old Ottoman Empire fell to its Young Turks in 1913. The assassination of Archduke Ferdinand of Austria in Serbia provoked the Great War a year later. The Bolsheviks overthrew the Russian Czars in 1917. The Irish revolution separated northern Unionists from southern Catholics. And the Austro-Hungarian Empire fell in 1918, shortly after its defeat in the bloodiest war in history.

The power of the British Empire peaked and fell into decline, outstripped by Germany and the United States, more adept at the processes of 20th-century industrialization. Across the old world new constitutions were drawn up that sought to enshrine the US ideal of 'government of the people, by the people, for the people'. For peasant, bourgeois and aristocratic people alike, this was cultural *terra nova* at the time and it was not at all clear how it would all hold together.

But that was only part of the challenge. While political upheavals tossed millions into a crisis of identity, in the worlds of science and philosophy other destabilizing shifts were underway. Physicists began to figure out that – at least at subatomic levels – reality was stranger than Newton's tidy laws had suggested. It seemed that matter was not a simple structure of atomic billiard balls, but could in fact act like either particles or waves and was not solid substance at all but a concentration of energy.

At almost the same time Jan Smuts (who for a time was Prime Minister in South Africa) was developing a system of non-reductionist thinking called 'holism' which proposed that the behaviour of an entity could not necessarily be inferred from observation of its constituent parts. It was an insight destined to transform how we think about human systems, challenging a reductionist tradition that stretched back to Descartes.

In 1930, some years before he was forced to flee Vienna, Freud wrote *Civilization and its Discontents* in which he examined the social and psychic costs of modernity. He pointed to a growing anxiety that seemed to permeate industrial societies. The poets too felt the seismic scale of the cultural turmoil. In what is surely the clearest call, William Butler Yeats in 1919 invoked images of terror and confusion. "What rough beast" he asked, "slouches towards Bethlehem to be born?"

Through the next decades a steady crescendo of voices was raised, at least in the West, from philosophy, psychology, the natural and social sciences and the humanities, pointing to a gradual unravelling of the social fabric we had taken as the natural order. It seemed that unless we could raise the capacity to respond we were heading for another "dark age".

By the 1970s, alarm was beginning to spread beyond the state of humanity to the state of the planet itself. In 1972 the Club of Rome warned that an interlocking pattern of global challenges threatened the capacity of the planet to sustain the consumption rate of an ever-increasing population. They calculated that the process would run into the buffers of physical resource constraints, the carrying capacity of a single planet. There were, in other words, 'Limits to Growth" (Meadows *et al.*, 1972).

But the warning went largely unheeded. In the years since the Second World War the mood had changed. Critics found the Club of Rome's analysis overly pessimistic and claimed that it discounted the power of technological innovation to produce resource efficiencies and new approaches that would free us from the predicted consequences of our actions.

Disquiet at another level was less easy to shake off. How would we be able to cope as human beings with an age of such rapid change, unimaginable new possibilities and the new threat of man-made planetary disaster – be it the slow degradation of the environment or the terrible prospect of 'mutually assured destruction' through the use of nuclear weapons?

Don Michael, a founder member of the Club of Rome who started his professional life as a policy adviser in Washington during the early years of the Cold War, began to turn his attention to this more pressing question. He feared for the consequences at a human level of living through a period of substantial turbulence in which individuals and societies were likely to lose their bearings. As he put it in the early 1970s:

> *All evidence suggests that, at least for the next*
> *couple of decades, the United States will be a highly*
> *turbulent society more likely than not, demoralizing*
> *itself into a splintered, culturally amorphous state of*
> *chronic social crises and catastrophe... All*
> *traditional [governance] approaches are likely to be*
> *relatively inadequate, and all new approaches are*
> *likely to have a high rate of failures as would any*
> *experiments performed under such relatively blind*
> *and complicated conditions.... We need to*

> *acknowledge that, somehow, we have discovered*
> *and are ensnared in a new wilderness, a new jungle,*
> *and that the skills that got us here are inadequate to*
> *get us out. Looking around us, we must*
> *acknowledge that we really are lost.*
>
> (Michael, 1973b)

This warning too proved too uncomfortable to be taken seriously. Michael found himself increasingly marginalized within groups thinking about the future for his dark vision. It broke faith with the American dream of untroubled progress and the long boom (Schwartz, Leyden & Hyatt, 1999).

Yet he continued to worry about the gap opening between the requirements of a rapidly changing global context and the skills and capacities we possess as individual human beings and collectives to meet them.

In the early 1990s, management theorist Peter Drucker, grounded in the concrete world of economics, governance and organizational practice, was still relatively upbeat about the future – although he too urged a rapid upgrading in our skills in organization, management, leadership and governance to respond to the radically new demands of a 'post-capitalist society'. Summing up his sense of the times he wrote:

> *Every few hundred years in Western history there*
> *occurs a sharp transformation. Within a few short*
> *decades, society rearranges itself – its worldview; its*
> *basic values; its social and political structures; its*
> *arts; its key institutions.... We are currently living*
> *through just such a transformation.*
>
> (Drucker, 1993)

This is surely where we find ourselves today, living inside a culture in flux (wherever we live) that is supporting neither us nor the planet terribly well. The three emergencies we described in the Introduction are ever present as objective threats and unconscious forces that frame our perceptions and aspirations. The dominant overarching narratives that might make sense of our world today are ambiguous at best, terminally gloomy at worst. The story of growth and development contradicts the story of resource constraint and the need for one-planet living. The story of connectedness, mobility and opportunity meets its shadow in the war on terror, the accelerating migration crisis and the clash of civilizations (Huntington, 1996). Every hopeful story inevitably excludes the dispossessed, the 'haves' always defined in relation to another group of 'have nots' whose plight, visible to all via non-stop media, becomes vividly more desperate all the time. Hovering over it all is the narrative of apocalypse: the ever more compelling evidence that the human species is already doomed by its previous folly.

From the highest levels of governance to the local level of families and individuals, incoherence is now endemic, generating states of high anxiety for individuals, for organizations and entire societies.

We scarcely know where to turn. We are struggling to address critical challenges, one by one, as they occur: bail out the financial system, negotiate emissions targets, set sustainable development goals, introduce democratic reform, reshape social policy. But the stakes keep on getting higher, the challenges the world is throwing at us more testing. And they all inter-relate. In Gwynne Dyer's (2008) telling metaphor, if avoiding nuclear war in the 20th century was the equivalent of getting our High School grades, addressing today's cascade of threats to life as we have lived it these past couple of hundred years will be more like 'sitting our finals'.

Disturbing the Psychosphere

The deeper story about what all this means for the patterning of consciousness, resilience and psychological capacity to cope has not attracted the attention it deserves. We are, after all, psychological beings. We expect our world to act in ways that our mental constructions and emotional responses have evolved to handle. We become deeply unsettled when that is not the case, when we sense a disruption in the psychosphere.[9]

That should not surprise us. Human consciousness is astoundingly complex. A healthy human brain contains over 200 million nerve cells or neurons, linked to one another via hundreds of trillions of synapses. Through this system flows information that drives both our actions and how we think and feel about them. But this arrangement is not fixed like wiring in a house with robust and resilient circuits that can be depended on to deliver the same results over time. It is more ephemeral, acting more like waves passing through crowds of individuals locking and unlocking their arms. One instant a connection is made and a signal travels, the next moment the connection is dropped and a new one made to another cell carrying another kind of input. In a vast, dynamic orchestration, sense is made and actions taken. Because memories of past actions persist, learning occurs. This makes the human brain one of the most complex systems we know.

Complex and delicate. Many of its systems – especially those connected to our emotional centres in the amygdala – are easily disturbed. For optimum mental functioning a certain degree of stability in the system is required, against which we notice important changes in patterns of coherence. Consciousness functions better when much of what it deals with can be set on default and taken for granted. It is the awareness of any "difference that makes a difference", as Gregory Bateson put it, that enables human beings to be alert to their circumstances, plan for the future and take effective action. When too much is in motion at the same time it is harder for the brain to separate what is important from what is just noise. Certainty becomes more fleeting, mistakes are made more frequently, anxiety increases.

Strictly speaking there is no such thing as a 'human brain' that can function separately from whole persons who have personalities, aspirations, hearts, stomachs, arms and legs. And there is also no such thing as a person separated from relationships, communities and institutions. Though all mammals have complex brains and smart monkeys can learn and memorize complex behavioural routines, they cannot reflect on their past actions and build a sense of shared meaning that persists beyond their presence. They participate in groups but they don't build cultures. It is humans who are the consummate institution builders. We have learned that, if patterns of life within human groups can be agreed upon and then taken for granted and transmitted to new arrivals, we have a better chance of dealing with unexpected challenges. We won't need to reinvent the wheel, or the farming techniques, or the family rituals. Institutionalization allows us to coordinate the action of groups with economy of effort and minimal social disruption or conflict; it also allows us to achieve something closer to our full potential (Ramachandran, 2011).

The combined result of today's era of a thousand revolutions is that long-standing frames of perception, cognition and patterns of life – *mentalities* – through which individual and group dignity and identity is preserved and existential anxieties managed – are breaking down on a global scale.[10] A mismatch has opened between mentalities that were adapted to their time and place and the demands of the world we now inhabit.

Some changes have occurred very quickly: the status of minorities and women for example. Laws and patterns of family life now take for granted the principle that women and men, regardless of race or creed, can expect the same rights, privileges and opportunities. And who could have imagined in 1973, when homosexuality was finally removed from the US Diagnostic and Statistical Manual as a mental disorder and anti-sodomy laws began to be gradually struck down around much of the Western world, that by 2019 gays and lesbians would be legally married, raising families and appointed to the clergy in mainstream Christian churches and a gay man would be Prime Minister of Ireland?

But the speed of these and other shifts and their acceptance by educated elites hides the deeper cultural story. The massive cultural changes of the 20th century have not been universally welcomed and the process of forming new social norms that will sustain these new ways of life without backlash or reaction is far from complete, even in relatively tolerant societies. Three examples give pause:

Homeschooling can be seen as an indicator of resistance to changing cultural norms. A substantial rise in the number of children in the US being schooled at home was propelled by a 1970s' Supreme Court ruling supporting the ban on prayer in schools. Christian parents reacted to what they felt as the tyranny of secular humanism by taking their children out of school and educating them themselves. By 2007 1.5 million children were being schooled at home. According to US Department of Education statistics, the most common reasons given for this are cultural – religion and values – with academic instruction a distant third (NCES, 2009).

Hate movements are another indicator of reaction to change too rapid to accommodate. Hate music arose in the UK in the 1970s as part of the skinhead subculture which emerged in reaction to the rapid influx of South Asian immigrants. At a time when urban violence in general is declining, violence against gays has increased 40% since gay marriage was legalized in the US and hate crimes against African Americans spiked after America elected its first black president.

Immigration is a smouldering issue in societies in the throes of cultural shifts. The editor of a north of England newspaper, Danny Lockwood (2011), explains the suffering in his home town of Dewsbury as: "A perfect storm. Our civic pride and governance has been systematically stripped away. Our industrial bedrock has gone. Mass immigration has brought all kinds of challenges that we haven't come close to understanding, let alone dealing with." The issue has continued to play through the UK's 'Brexit' referendum and beyond.

A world away, in the US, feelings about immigration also run high. A country made up of immigrants is deeply divided. Donald Trump based his campaign for the presidency on a hard-edged, anti-immigration platform, stirring up anti-immigrant fervour at his rallies with chants of "build that wall" (referring to a proposal to construct a physical barrier along the US southern border). Almost immediately after taking office he enacted laws to block immigration from Islamic countries and countermanded an Obama-era bill that permitted young immigrants brought to the

US as children to access benefits such as healthcare, driver's licences, in-state tuition at college and a path to full citizenship.

Nativism – an extreme strand of American thought stretching back to the early colonists – is on the rise. It is heard in campaign pledges to "take our country back" and in doubts freely expressed about whether former President Obama, whose father was an immigrant, could be a real American. At the same time there has been intense opposition to these moves and the mid-term elections in 2018 saw a big shift with Democrats taking back control of the House of Representatives and more women and minorities elected than ever before.

In these transitional times we are losing our bearings. The real, the conceptual and the existential emergencies are showing up on a cultural scale (Leicester & O'Hara, 2007).

Culture Matters

We have to try to make sense of today's powerful times at the cultural level. We are a culturally created and culture creating species. We all live, grow up, find our place in and are socialized by cultures: the patterns of shared experience that shape (and are shaped by) our lives. And whenever external circumstances undergo radical and confounding change, it is felt at a cultural level as well as in the lives of individuals.

This is often not obvious. In the more individualistic Western cultures[11] of Europe and North America people are mostly oblivious to the ways their behaviour expresses a particular culture. In the US, for example, a sports fan's adrenaline rises as the running back carries the football a few yards down the field. His British guest remains unmoved and wonders what the fuss is about. Afterwards, if they discuss their different experiences of the game, neither is likely to refer to the years of cultural messages surrounding them at every move as the reason for their different physiological responses to the same event.

The Japanese-born Shinobu Kitayama, Professor of Psychology at the University of Michigan and considered one of the leaders in the field of cultural psychology, has shown just how deep the effects of culture go. He and his colleagues have studied the way brain waves react differently when Asian and American students are shown the same scene. Differences have been found in most of the core areas of psychological functioning. These patterns are modifiable to some degree – we couldn't learn anything new if they weren't. But it is now clear that some things we learn early in life become part of the basic neurological and psychological scaffolding of our being and everything we subsequently encounter must be addressed with reference to this early foundational experience.

Culture also colours perception. An Australian aboriginal discerns signs in his or her landscape that suggest the presence of water below the surface: signs that a newcomer simply does not see. The Arab musician hears and can repeat separations of tones that most Westerners cannot. And if bridging the gap between cultures can therefore feel difficult, it is even more so across historical eras. How are secular moderns to fully understand the minds of Roman citizens who enjoyed the spectacle of lions tearing apart captured slaves in the Colosseum, or of pious Spanish missionaries who put to death countless aboriginals in the Americas immediately after baptizing them, or even closer in time, but every bit as distant in the sense of what is normal or acceptable, 19th-century British miners who sent seven-year-olds to work in the mines? To understand such alien actions we must enter a different cosmology – a comprehensive view of reality – where such actions made sense.

Westerners have come to think of themselves as sovereign individuals who 'have' a culture. This individualistic sense of self seriously underestimates the degree to which culture and psychology are inextricably interpenetrated. Most of the anchors of meaning about what matters to us arise from within particular cultural settings. Culture will tell us what it is to be 'successful', how to express our values in context, how to encounter people not like ourselves. It will shape our identity, whether we choose to conform or rebel. As we grow into culturally expected ways of being and acting by participating in family life, governance, education, economics and art we reproduce the conditions that will 'cultivate' the next generation.

Richard Shweder (1991) suggests that we all need a set of core storylines – elements that need to pervade all aspects of life from domestic arrangements to civic institutions to religious beliefs and practices – to account successfully for what he calls the "existential facts of life". At a minimum these include answers to questions such as: Who are we and where do we come from (are we children of God, of human parents, subjects of the King, sovereign individuals)? How should things (like the economy, education or kinship systems) be organized? What is the relationship between human beings and nature (are we part of it, victims of it, above it)? Why do some people have more material benefits than others? Why is there a difference between 'our' way of life and 'theirs'?

The specific answers to such core questions differ widely from society to society. But in stable societies debates about the deeper assumptions underpinning reality are rare. Whether based in religion, myth, science, politics or the arts, social harmony and collective success depend on a fair amount of consensus about 'the way things are'.

In the best of times in stable societies the answers to these questions are transmitted tacitly and coherently through each and every cultural act and provide the taken-for-granted symbols and metaphors, conceptual understandings and habits of life, that enable us to get along without undue conflict or strife.

But what happens when those cultural patterns are in flux? When the old rules no longer function well because they are not up to the new levels of complexity, uncertainty and rapid change in society, but new rules have not been written? When the falcon cannot hear the falconer? When a stable culture starts to collapse the challenge is no longer just external: it becomes existential.

Stay Hungry, Stay Foolish, Don't Settle

There are grounds for hope. The human story is full of examples of occasions when, out of the depths of crisis, some individual or group takes a bold creative step which changes not only the rules but the game itself. The adaptive ingenuity that has made human beings such an extraordinary evolutionary success suggests that when we are challenged beyond our current capacities we may rise to meet the challenge with some radical innovation. There is no reason to believe our creative days are behind us.

We also know that cultural evolution can take place rapidly. In the fifty years between the invention of the printing press in 1450 and the end of the 15th century, for example, over a thousand printing offices, in 350 towns, had printed 30,000 titles covering topics from the Bible to the classics, humanistic poetry, philosophy and politics. Whilst this was the result in the first instance of technological innovation, its greatest impact was cultural. It made it possible for the first time for people of modest means to gain an education, to grasp more of the complexity and wonder of their world, and to develop the capacity to act as cultural leaders themselves (Füssel, 2003).

The idea that not only individuals and societies but also entire cultures have histories is a relatively new concept and is a product of our astonishing new capacity to collect and analyse large amounts of information. For the first time it is possible to trace the history of human societies down to the minutiae of what they ate or what kind of stitches they used in their needlework. We can recognize times when deep changes occur in how people see their world, the way they understand reality and the way they believe society should be governed. When cultures begin to shift, their core narratives, symbols, rituals, institutions, laws, expectations and values and conceptual frames change or take on new meanings.

One source of hope therefore is that many of the elders in

society today – captains of industry, leaders of governments, teachers and public intellectuals – have lived through such a time. They carry in their bones (and possibly still in their hearts) the experience of growing up in the excitement and uncertainty of the cultural turbulence of the 1960s onwards.

In the US the relatively solid cultural norms of the immediate post-war era were challenged by a generation who questioned the values of a 'military industrial complex' that sent poor and middle-class youth to war while the sons of the elites stayed home, in school, got advanced degrees and got rich. Anti-war protestors joined civil rights activists, feminists and campus radicals in teach-ins, sit-ins and consciousness-raising groups where the guiding frameworks of culture were unpacked and critically evaluated.

Though the stated intention of these movements was revolution in the direction of expanded social justice for minorities, women and exploited classes, the activities these young people engaged in provided both warp and woof for consciousness at a level of greater psychological capacity that began to lay the foundation for a new culture.

The 'hidden curriculum' of modernity was under review not only as an intellectual exercise but as a reflective practice. Participants in women's groups studying the history of gender politics by reading Simone de Beauvoir, for example, not only became literate about social theory but also demanded different kinds of relationships with their boyfriends. In a myriad settings, addressing race, sexuality, the environment, conceptual framing, language, love, ethics, politics, curriculum, governance, economics, mental health, personal growth, consciousness, consumerism, toxic chemicals, organic food, family structures, work, art and popular culture, young people were engaged in a comprehensive reassessment of modernity and in the process developing new capacities for life in the postmodern context. When young men working to end the draft, civil rights workers standing up for racial justice, college students demanding a more relevant curriculum, signed on to feminist Carol Hanisch's observation that "the personal is political", they were for the first time pointing out the inseparability of psychological capacity and political arrangements. They were becoming a new kind of person within new kinds of cultural arrangements.

Not everyone welcomed these strange new voices and many found their heresies ridiculous, even dangerous. News coverage of the day offers stories of nude 'streakers', violent rock concerts, love-ins, and warnings that such permissiveness was a threat to civilization. Traditionalists found their certainties and their deep values challenged and often egregiously scorned by those voices eager to make the case for a new culture by pointing out the iniquities of the old. Campaigns arose to push back against the transgressive tide, clamping down on sex education, values-clarification programmes and sensitivity training in schools. Some of the more doctrinaire habits and extreme stances were dismissed as examples of Mao-style 'political correctness', anti-feminists warned that the Equal Rights Amendment robbed women of their privileges as 'dependent wives' and bombs were set at birth control clinics.

In the 1980s all across America, traditionalists who were determined to regain control over a culture that in their view was moving in the wrong direction supported 'stealth candidates' for local school boards and town councils. But the wave could not be stopped as women and minorities showed up in previously white male bastions like business, higher education, law, government and medicine in greater numbers, bringing with them not only their demographic diversity but also new kinds of consciousness – the product of their transformative experience in social movements.

Over the next years compromises were struck and new laws enacted that took the edge off some of the sources of protest and at the same time set a new stage for cultural transformation that is still under way. The generation who refused to be "bent, stapled or mutilated", who at the 1968 Democratic National Convention in Chicago reminded riot police that "the whole world is watching", who went on spiritual pilgrimages to find enlightenment and turned up in 1970 for the first Earth Day are mostly still with us, but they have mellowed a bit over time as adult demands take priority.

Yet the psychological capacities forged during their formative years in fights for racial justice, anti-war demonstrations, meditation, LSD, commune life, organic farming, women's collectives, all demanding the unfreezing of established patterns of life and an embracing of the emergent and the hopeful, is still alive in them. While the culture as a whole maintains its resistance and in some ways has strengthened the pressures to conform – sometimes to an extreme degree – every so often established leaders can still be found recalling the new consciousness and explicitly celebrating it.

The last few years have seen the gathering power of reaction sweep across the world, the rise of the political and religious right wing, sometimes with extremist parties gaining elected power and anti-democratic movements gaining strength in previously democratic societies. Even so, we notice that wherever these reactive currents emerge they also stimulate the renewal of action and energy in a generation that wants to sustain a transformative momentum. Three million women and supporters march in Washington DC in response to Donald Trump's election, hundreds of thousands more in the UK take to the streets to support the European Union, across Europe young people mobilize against climate threats, the entire population of New Zealand joins an open-hearted expression of shared grief after a gunman mowed down Muslims at worship, and gay pride parades are now sponsored by companies which would not have employed gays a generation ago. Cultural changes driven by the values that emerged in the 1960s are alive in the children and grandchildren of that wave.

Apple founder Steve Jobs was typical of the 1960s' generation, openly acknowledging his 'inner hippie' and creating a company that, aside from all its traditional commercial success, retained a space (at least for him while he was with us) to express it. His famous commencement address to Stanford graduates in 2005 would not have been out of place in the 1960s. He spoke not about what the graduates in front of him should do with their lives, how they might take their place in the established cultural order, but rather how they should grow as individuals. "Have the courage to follow your heart and intuition", he said, "they somehow already know what you truly want to become". To a group of young people living in a culture in flux his message was simply to keep looking, keep following the path of the heart, keep trusting in the future: "Don't settle... Stay hungry. Stay foolish."[12]

These words above all were picked up after his untimely death in October 2011 as expressing the essence of Jobs's life. For those still wrestling with the need for cultural change they offered a different way of looking at a world of baffling complexity and fearful challenge. They were inspirational and his millennial heirs have run with them, transforming everything they touch as they engage with the challenges of their times. With an insistence on sovereignty, self-determination and innovation they are reshaping their culture. Following Jobs's clarion call, they "don't settle" for outworn concepts and conventional understandings, demonstrating in action that we do not have to be overwhelmed by the complexity and messiness of the times. We can instead learn and grow through it, and in the process live fulfilled lives. We can rise to the occasion.

CHAPTER 2:

GROWING WITH THE TIMES

Defensive Denial

Our assertion is that we all now need to grow in order to flourish in today's powerful times. The good news is that we know a great deal about how such growth occurs. The bad news is that much of what we know explains the strength of our resistance. In practice, current levels of complexity and incoherence produce high levels of anxiety which in turn provoke three distinct individual and societal responses: defensive denial, chaotic collapse, or growth and transformation. How might we trigger the last?

There is a reason why Jobs's advice to stay hungry, foolish and unsettled is not the conventional wisdom. It clearly places great psychological demands on the individual. The attraction of the opposite state – security, satisfaction, and expertise – is almost irresistible. Indeed, when these parallel virtues come under threat – when we feel hungry, foolish, unsettled – it usually generates a sense of anxiety. This is a potent force in human affairs.

As will be clear from the previous chapter, we believe today's level of cultural disturbance is making us feel anxious: all of us some of the time and some of us all of the time. Sadly the instinctive response to anxiety – in individuals, organizations and entire societies – is likely to be defensive denial, a distortion of reality to make it conform to our pre-existing expectations. In his classic studies on cognitive dissonance, Leon Festinger (1957) showed that, when people are presented with a situation that contradicts what they have previously taken as a certainty, they may resort to creative psychological strategies to hold their anxiety at bay.

Aesop's confident fox, unable despite his best efforts to reach the luscious looking grapes in the fable, avoids feeling like a failure by deciding the grapes were probably sour anyway. No failure, just a wise change in direction justified by the imagined evidence. We humans are even more creative in our defences. We can deny the uncertainty and the challenge, discredit its validity, rationalize, disavow, reinforce the familiar, recruit fellow travellers, shut out and often demonize the unknown – in other words resist. These defensive moves, conscious and unconscious, individual and collective, are geared towards maintaining old patterns of coherence on which we have come to rely and avoid having to face and adapt to a new reality.

Examples are not hard to find. The Japanese phenomenon of hikikomori – young men (typically) who refuse to leave their rooms to engage in a world that they find overwhelming; increasing xenophobia and anti-immigrant racism in the face of shifting demographics; denying the reality of the HIV virus in South Africa; looking the other way on paedophilia in the Roman Catholic Church; accepting the 'alternative facts' offered by fake news; attempts to discredit the science of climate change; finding scapegoats in immigrant and minority ethnic groups, and so on. If all else fails to tune out the discomfort there is always the escape to distraction or, as social psychologist Neil Postman (1985) puts it, "amusing ourselves to death".

All these instances carry the hallmarks of defensive denial. They are attempts to hold back our awareness of a world of disruptive change for as long as possible by binding the private and collective anxiety that accompanies it. The strategies are mostly unconscious and appear as a normal default defence against too much unsettling information and rising psychological uncertainty. Because they are unconscious, we usually believe the distortion and are hard to convince otherwise. We see what we want to believe, rather than believe what we actually see.

Though costly in terms of psychological effort and energy, these defensive strategies can be successful in fending off anxiety until conditions return to stability. But if the stance has to be maintained over an extended period the psychic costs mount. It becomes ever more effortful to seal off disturbing reality in order to maintain some semblance of familiarity.

When the defence becomes habitual it can itself become a source of incoherence – and we enter the realm that psychologists consider neurotic. We become less and less in touch with the full implications of our reality, engage in maladaptive, ineffective strategies that fail to bring the desired results and we are less able to bring our capacities to bear on the challenge at hand. Holding on in the face of increasing discomfort makes us eager for distraction, easy prey for despotic leaders, and vulnerable to anyone or anything promising the restoration of certainty, simplicity and continued 'progress' in troubled times. Neuroticism has always driven a bull market in fool's gold.

Even more problematic are responses that involve losing our connection with reality altogether. This can be the pattern people fall into when the psychological effort to maintain effective denial becomes too great. The next step is not enlightenment but collapse. People fall into a delusional or fantasy world where they make up a reality that is tolerable for them, however distorted it may be from the point of view of most others. In that unreal world they can give up the struggle to make sense of the complexities around them; they can tune out, get lost in their fear and rage, 'eat drink and be merry', secure in their delusional belief that they will be fine.

Events like the mass homicide-suicides in Jonestown, genocides like those in Rwanda and Darfur, the Nazi Holocaust, suicide bombings and many other forms of religious violence, the tortured logic of paranoid killers 'going postal', self-destructive actions such as drug abuse, anorexia and self-mutilation reveal the destructive power of this psychotic level of defence against unbearable levels of anxiety.

The news items of the day are replete with examples and add to the febrile nature of the times. As noted earlier, mental health statistics point to a global epidemic of serious mental distress along a continuum from mild distress to deep despair or debilitating psychic disorientation.

The Growth Response

Whilst they appear to be a powerful default, defensive denial or chaotic collapse are not the only possible response to fluid times. Rollo May spoke for most psychoanalysts in seeing the negative consequences of cultural anxiety. But he also sensed the potential for growth:

> *When a culture is caught in the profound*
> *convulsions of a transitional period the individuals*
> *in the society understandably suffer spiritual and*
> *emotional upheaval; and finding that the accepted*
> *mores and ways of thought no longer yield security,*
> *they tend either to sink into dogmatism and*
> *conformism, giving up awareness, or are forced to*
> *strive for a heightened self-consciousness by which*
> *to become aware of their new existence with new*
> *conviction and on new bases.* (1983, p.57)

There is indeed ample evidence that under some circumstances, which we will explore in greater depth later in this book, we can as individual persons or in groups adopt a more growth-oriented stance, neither denying nor tuning out the confusing and overwhelming complexity. Instead we can sit with it, engage with it, develop and grow through it. In some situations, when conditions are right, we can transcend the apparent chaos and expand into something genuinely new. We adapt to the times, allowing the new circumstances to call forth capacities, individually and collectively, that we did not know we possessed. This is the transformative response.

This too is a perfectly natural response, if we allow it. Chaos, even confusion, is intolerable for the human psyche for more than a short time. By virtue of our neurological make-up, humans are unavoidably meaning – and coherence – seekers. Over a hundred thousand years of evolution our species has addressed its challenges not by avoiding them but by growing into them and adapting to them. But just because it is our nature does not mean it is easy. And it could have been otherwise. Evolutionary biologists report that at one time there were at least four different species of humans living in wandering bands, cooking their food, revering their dead and making art. Only one – us – successfully adapted to the serial challenges to survival by learning what was needed in changing circumstances.

Faced with demands for which no capacity existed in the past we have overcome the deficit by developing new ideas and inventions that have permitted adaptation – and that in turn have brought new challenges. Stone tools, then metal tools, ceramics, chemistry, wheels, calendars, settled communities, money, writing, animal domestication, ploughs, seed selection and crop rotation were inventions to solve specific problems and changed the future of the human species. Thus over time we have evolved the technology-based civilizations with high levels of organizational, economic and social complexity and rapid change that exist in the developed world today.

We have created macro-cultures, national sub-cultures, micro-cultures, hybrid cultures, temporary cultures and counter-cultures, with fixed identities, fluid identities, multiple identities – all as responses to the kaleidoscopic contexts of human lives.

We are, it is clear, a self-made species. Unlike non-conscious creatures, whose development is largely controlled by genetically established programmes or instincts with little left to individual creativity, human development is the result of human achievement. In its essence it is a process of growth and learning that enables us to expand personal mental and organizational capacities to keep pace with and thrive on the higher levels of complexity we seem destined to create.

How We Grow

So how exactly does this process of growth occur? It turns out we know quite a lot about how human beings learn and develop, much of it very old wisdom indeed. Biologically the brain of a child born today in New York City comes equipped with basically the same structure and function as a child born in a Stone Age encampment, modern Shanghai or in an Amazonian hunter-gatherer's village. Each child starts out with the same set of mental potentialities with which to meet their world.

We in the West have paid a lot of attention to the question of how a human child progresses from the simple cognition of infancy to the fully developed capacities of adulthood. In the East the story does not stop there: practices continue throughout life aimed at the achievement of levels of consciousness beyond adulthood to sagehood and ultimately enlightenment.

This story of stage-based development is key to a whole host of models of lifelong growth: spiral dynamics based on the work of Clare Graves and elaborated by Don Beck, the integral theory of Ken Wilber and Susanne Cook-Greuter, neo-Piagetian cognitive theories championed by Jane Loevinger, Robert Kegan and Mihaly Csikszentmihalyi, the existential humanist analysis of Carol Ryff, or Marxist-influenced theories advanced by Paulo Freire and Lev Vygotsky – to name some of the currently most influential. And before them Freud, Erikson, Jung, Piaget, Kohlberg, Maslow and Rogers offered theories of how human consciousness matures from infanthood to old age.

Our understanding of how people grow is thus well established. And we are growing all the time. Contemporary cognitive and neurological research makes it pretty clear that human 'being' is actually an open, continuous process of transformation. What we think of as 'a person', neatly walled off from the world as a separate fixed identity, is better thought of as 'autopoiesis' (self-creation) – the emergent consequence of intentional interactions between inherently meaning-seeking creatures and their social world.

Children enter their culturally distinct native worlds with a nervous system primed to perceive, respond and learn. Over time this open process of engagement constructs the developing person's consciousness.

From studies of development in adults across different populations we find that as people move through childhood and adulthood to old age there are discernible shifts in mental complexity. Though there is considerable variation among populations at any age, the demarcation between levels represents different 'meaning systems' – ways of perceiving, interpreting and understanding the world. The meaning system through which we view the world will influence what we communicate, what we understand and how we act. There are key markers in the research that signal distinct orders of mental complexity: Robert Kegan and Lisa Lahey (2009) call them the socialized mind, the self-authoring mind and the self-transforming mind (see the table below, adapted from their book).

The socialized mind
• We are shaped by the definitions and expectations of our personal environment
• Our self coheres by its alignment with, and loyalty to, that which it identifies
• This can express itself primarily in our relationships with people, with 'schools of thought' (our ideas and beliefs), or both
The self-authoring mind
• We are able to step back enough from the social environment to generate an internal 'seat of judgement' or personal authority that evaluates and makes choices about external expectations
• Our self coheres by its alignment with its own belief system/ ideology/personal code; by its ability to self-direct, take stands, set limits, and create and regulate its boundaries on behalf of its own voice
The self-transforming mind
• We can step back from and reflect on the limits of our own ideology or personal authority; see that any one system or self-organization is in some way partial or incomplete; be friendlier towards contradiction and opposites; seek to hold on to multiple systems rather than projecting all but one on to the other
• Our self coheres through the ability not to confuse internal consistency with wholeness or completeness, and through alignment with the dialectic rather than with either pole.

Experts differ about whether these capacities represent a universal developmental hierarchy in reasoning and rationality, or vary due to personality, gender, ethnicity, educational level, life-style and life circumstances. With the caveat that we should not over-generalize, there is fairly wide agreement that distinct habits of mind can be identified among adults. Not everyone operates at the same level of mental complexity and there are distinct cognitive and emotional styles co-existing in any society.

Getting Beyond Defensive Denial

Estimates differ about the proportion of any population operating at each of these different levels. Nevertheless, a consensus seems to exist among developmental psychologists that most of us operate at the level of the 'socialized mind', making sense of the world and developing strategies for living based on received truth and non-reflective personal opinion. Those who study more advanced levels of consciousness – usually described as wisdom – report that actualization of such levels in individuals is quite rare. One study found that when given vignettes of complex situations calling for a wise response only eleven individuals out of a group of 250 met the criteria.[13]

This segmentation was unremarkable in the industrial age, an age of relative stability, where accepting the interpretations and understandings passed down from traditional authorities could provide a sufficient basis for success. But now the world is far more demanding for all of us. Robert Kegan (1994) concluded in his influential work that we were already, towards the end of the last century, 'in over our heads' and struggling to cope with the mental demands of modern life. Creativity guru Mihaly Csikszentmihalyi (1993) calls us "half-formed" and wonders if we will grow up before we destroy ourselves and our planetary homeland.

The pressures of 'always on' globalization and the heightened competition of turbo-capitalism are showing up all around us, not least in the business organizations that shape our working lives. Zielenziger's *Shutting Out The Sun* (2006) points to a deep social malaise afflicting Japan as a result of its failure to absorb the turbulences of a post-manufacturing world. It has the highest suicide rate amongst the developed nations and the lowest birth rate. "Contemporary Japan is at peace, but everyone who lives there knows something is wrong. Like its crown princess, the nation and its young people seem to be on the edge of a nervous breakdown."

A litany of statistics from around the world offers little encouragement.[14] It points to what amounts to a global epidemic of mental distress, showing up in suicide rates, alcoholism and drug use, divorce rates, domestic and other violence, not to mention the half billion people suffering some kind of serious mental distress that qualifies as a 'mental illness' under the World Health Organization definitions.

It is clear we need dramatically to increase our capacities across the board in order to become more comfortable living in today's world. A cursory glance at the market for executive recruitment bears this out. Routine management positions now ask for a range of competencies that were once associated with the most senior roles while job specifications for senior managers and leaders have added layer upon layer of desirable skills and experience to keep up with the multi-faceted nature of a changing world.

The result is that senior roles now demand a portfolio of skills and human capacities little short of the miraculous. A special feature on business education in the *Financial Times,* for example, listed the following desirable characteristics for corporate leaders: "having a fiercely sharp intellect, being a 'black belt' in people skills, being genuinely intellectually curious about the world, while also boasting superb energy levels and a certain personal humility." (Stern, 2006)

We have reached the point where we are asking for super-human capacities in our leaders and senior managers: everything short of walking on water. Highly evolved human beings are now required to enable our organizations to operate effectively.

The problem is that evolving these kinds of capacities is not always easy and we often try to avoid it if we can. It is significant that after a decade of urging us to learn our way to higher mental capacities, Robert Kegan's more recent work has concentrated not on development but on the barriers to it, what he calls 'immunity to change'. (Kegan & Lahey 2009)

Albert Hirschman's classic study *The Rhetoric of Reaction* (1991) conducted an exhaustive search for defensive strategies in politics and policy-making, exploring the kinds of arguments we typically deploy to resist change and maintain the status quo. He identified three dominant tropes: perversity, futility and jeopardy. In other words, we tend to argue that whatever change is proposed will have the opposite of its intended effect, or it will have no effect, or it will put in jeopardy good things that have been achieved already under the existing system. These are the familiar defensive routines of resistance throughout the ages.

At a deeper psychological level the literature lists several other instinctive defence mechanisms, many of which are now household words: denial, which we have already met – failing to acknowledge some new experience; projection – ascribing to others an unacceptable thought or impulse of one's own; rationalization – making up an alternative, more palatable explanation for an action; reaction formation – overreacting negatively to something one unconsciously desires so as to keep it from getting too close; distortion – misreading a situation so as to create an alternative meaning that does not challenge one's existing sense of order.

What these mechanisms have in common is that they bind or control anxiety by filtering experience to make it fit existing meaning systems. Like children who believe that if they place a bag over their head they become invisible to the bogey man, we calm ourselves down with adult equivalents. The last few decades have brought to popular attention the concept of cognitive biases and perceptual fallacies as an explanation for why we make decisions that don't conform to mathematical logic. These also serve unconsciously to simplify our world of boundless choices. We all do this. If we didn't, our lives would indeed be overwhelming. But when the psychological defence or bias takes over and becomes the default response in the face of most novel experience, then we move into the realm of neurosis. When our mindsets are on defensive autopilot and we keep on acting and thinking as if the world were not changing, then our range of adaptive action shrinks. As R. D. Laing (1971) put it:

> *The range of what we think and do is limited by*
> *what we fail to notice. And because we fail to notice*
> *that we fail to notice, there is little we can do to*
> *change, until we notice how failing to notice shapes*
> *our thoughts and deeds.*

In psychological terms 'failing to notice' is a 'neurotic' response to conceptual emergency. It defends the psyche. And it operates by default.

We can see this in our day-to-day responses as the fragile, tightly coupled systems on which we rely start to fracture and anxiety rises. We place our faith in leaders who claim to be able to get the complex systems on which we rely 'back under control'. Or risk managers who analyse mountains of data to reassure us against the unpredictable. Or leaders who tell us that we can carry on as normal in spite of tectonic global change.

And to an extent we can. But the enduring stability of our systems, which is a strength during times of relative calm, becomes a weakness in an environment of rapid change. Assets become liabilities and vice versa. Dimitry Orlov (2008) had just that experience during the collapse of the Soviet Union. The store that lost efficiency by keeping a large inventory before the collapse, for example, found itself the only one with stock to sell afterwards.

So it is that for the most part, by failing to notice we are also failing to develop the capacities and the 21st-century competencies of persons of tomorrow. Our default is to stay safe and reinforce old habits. If we don't take the risk, we will find ourselves stuck in a level of mind inadequate to the demands of the times. But, if we understand that the existential challenge is also an existential opportunity, we can turn neurotic defensiveness into transformative learning.

CHAPTER 3:

COMPETENCE IN THE 21ST CENTURY

The Full Development of the Human Personality

We have described both the challenge of the times and the nature of the growth process it demands of us. So it would be natural at this stage of the argument to expect a neat list of 21st-century competencies that will make us fit for the future.

The second part of this book will indeed discuss the kinds of qualities, capacities and competencies that 'persons of tomorrow', well adapted for today's fluid times, display. But any such enumeration risks feeding a set of late-20th-century cultural norms that have grown up around how we frame 'competencies' and how to develop them – norms that themselves need to be re-examined. We live in a culture that is in thrall to the twin reductionist gods of economics and behaviourism. It will be very difficult to develop 21st-century competencies so long as our systems, processes and institutions remain dominated by these 20th-century mindsets.

It was not always thus. From the insights of Freud in the early years of the 20th century onwards, we have made powerful progress in understanding the human condition. And that progress has been matched by a parallel facility in converting cultural anxiety over time into the growth response, developing new capacities for the times.

The cultural crisis that opened the 20th century – the advance of our modern industrial/technological economy – called into question previous patterns of stability and conceptions of what constituted a good life. The collapse of male identity in a world of automation and office work, for example, triggered a whole set of cultural institutions to deal with the resulting ennui – the boy scouts, DIY, militarism, English-style public schools, a revival of medievalism and the courtly code, self-help and psychoanalysis. Though apparently distinct and unrelated, these cultural inventions were parts of a diverse response to a common perturbation – the emasculating effects of industrialization (Jackson Lears, 1994).

As the first half of the century progressed, the thrust of this movement was towards reclaiming a vision of human potential and dignity in an age dominated by the wonders of technology and new machines. Words like freedom, potential, transcendence, love, awe, dignity, being, consciousness, meaning, joy, pleasure, compassion, populated the titles of books exploring the outer reaches of human possibility. The playing out of these efforts to transform cultural anxiety into growth took several decades. But they ushered in an era after the Second World War that was influenced by a more capacious view of the 'self-actualizing' individual, no longer ensnared by the demands of the economy and its machines.

That view was captured in the 1948 Universal Declaration of Human Rights – a highly influential cultural document. It enshrined the right to an education "directed to the full development of the human personality", the right "to enjoy the arts and to share in scientific advancement and its benefits", and observed that for any person it is only in community that "the free and full development of his personality is possible".

Seventy years on, the Universal Declaration looks like a high-water mark. Since then, and with gathering pace since the market liberalization of the 1980s, we have seen a narrowing of perspective. We seem to have moved back to a deficit model that puts faith not in boundless human potential, but rather our ability to learn specific new skills – just in time – to fulfil productive roles in society.

The Neurotic Pursuit of Competence

The pursuit of increased, specific competence has proceeded

apace. Whether in order to respond to exponential growth in information, the possibilities of new technologies and new competition (in business) or new levels of disillusion, fear and distress (in society), the search has been on for some time now to develop the new competencies necessary to adjust to today's world.

But that search has become increasingly neurotic. In contrast with the expansive view of human capacity enshrined in the Universal Declaration, our drive has turned technocratic: mastering more and more specialized knowledge and specific competencies to fulfil specific roles in an ever more complex economic and social system. A 25-year-old study from Henley Management College (Institute of Directors, 1994), for example, lists nearly 40 'core competencies' for directors:

Strategy, Perception and Decision-making
Perspective (helicopter)
Organizational awareness
Strategic awareness
Vision
Imagination
Judgement
Decisiveness
Change-oriented
Analytical understanding
Information collection
Detail consciousness
Numerical interpretation
Problem analysis
Critical faculty
Communication
Oral communication
Listening
Openness
Written communication
Interacting with others
Coordinating

Assertiveness
Impact
Persuasiveness
Motivating others
Sensitivity
Flexibility
Board management
Planning
Organizing
Delegating
Appraising
Developing directors
Achieving results
Energy
Achievement-motivation
Determination
Independence
Risk-taking
Business sense
Resilience
Integrity

Another more recent report – *Thriving in the 21st Century* – is, as one would expect, more comprehensive, listing 81 relevant "competencies, qualities and attributes" ranging from "scanning and interpreting the environment" to "finding others to work with who complement your strengths" (Dods & Andrews, 2010). Each new study builds on the last, adding 'new' discoveries to the list.

Though certainly not wrong – these competencies are undoubtedly useful and if mastered would enhance a person's ability to perform successfully in 21st-century work settings – the lists themselves betray a fundamentally neurotic response to today's cultural crisis. They are almost compulsive attempts to deny that things are unmanageable, offering instead the comforting promise that all can be mastered if only one has these skills.

Seeing the edifice of our existing culture crumbling, and the anxiety and pain this is causing in a generation trying to keep up, the competence cataloguers rush to reinforce every bending beam, close every fissure – each weakness addressed with its own specific remedy. And each of these new specialist competencies spawns a separate module in a degree course, a tailored workshop from a training provider, or a raft of self-help books and instructional videos produced by individuals who are certain that they themselves exhibit all these competencies in full measure.

One consequence is that in the last few decades the demands of all professions have become infinitely more complicated. When the famous Powerpoint slide (Bumiller, 2010) analysing the war in Afghanistan surfaced in *The New York Times*, showing an almost indecipherable mess map, millions of senior managers recognized their own overwhelming situations.[41] Even accounting – not a field usually associated in the public mind with rapid change – has gone from not being a profession at all at the beginning of the 20ᵗʰ century to being so complicated that 10,000 pages are needed to explain its core principles today (Segal, 2010).

Some of the most vigorous debates now among academics and professional bodies are about what has to be dropped from the ever-expanding canon to make room for new essential knowledge. Each new requirement ups the ante in the credentialing game, drives new demands for continuing education, and adds to the pressure and expense of making it as a professional with the necessary competencies.

For a while it works. A weekend away on a training course or a new MBA reduces anxiety and boosts one's sense of adequacy. But once back in the real world of uncertainty a creeping sense of bewilderment returns – only now expectations of competence have been raised a notch or two higher. Like a drug addict whose last fix has worn off, the sense of being in over one's head returns. The remedy, in other words, is amplifying the ailment.

Each new requirement, each addition to the modern curriculum or to the list of required competencies for the job, adds to the sense of overwhelm and inadequacy and further deepens the cultural crisis. Hence what we are seeing today in the worlds of education and training is a kind of 'iatrogenesis' – doctor-induced disease. The psychological assumptions that drive these industries and associated policy-making are in practice making the situation worse.

Nudging Ourselves to Competence

Fundamentally what matters is the view we hold of the person: who we are and what we are capable of becoming.

Over a hundred years ago Frederick Winslow Taylor's scientific management inspired both Henry Ford and Vladimir Lenin with the idea that breaking every job action into small simple steps that can be measured and analysed would lead to improved efficiency. So it proved in practice – and this style is now all-pervasive in our modern world, including in education.

It has brought huge improvements in efficiency, productivity and the effective management of ever more complex processes. But what is less obvious is the particular view of personhood that Taylor's theory and its 21st-century descendants have enshrined as the cultural norm. This is the behaviourist view, inherited from the Enlightenment: that human beings are in essence no more than autonomous agents motivated to act in predictable ways by prompts which provoke responses aimed at predetermined outcomes.

Prompts can be anything from a rumbling stomach to a promotion: to which the responses might be ordering a pizza or moving the family to Chicago. This logic has driven industrial age thinking since the 18th century and accepts implicitly a simple and direct relationship between causes and effects even in the complex lives of persons, groups and communities. Administer the right prompt and you will get the desired response.

Human beings can thus be managed through the careful application of efficient design coupled with appropriate rewards and punishments. The role of leadership and management is to design efficient systems, monitor outcomes and reward success.

In essence this view suggests that what we need are smart systems to compensate for dumb humans. It is not a mindset likely to foster the development of persons of tomorrow.

Nor in our view is the new field of behavioural economics, which holds an even more pessimistic view of human potential. One prominent advocate, Dan Ariely (2008), a Professor of Psychology and Behavioural Economics at Duke University, considers human behaviour to be "predictably irrational". He describes people as "myopic", "confused", "not knowing what they want" and offers behavioural economics as a "crutch" to deal with the world (Brinn & Duckworth, 2008).

Nobel prize-winner Daniel Kahneman (2011), the godfather of behavioural economics and a regular feature of the TED talk circuit, has compiled a vast amount of research on the degree to which humans make irrational and erroneous choices. His favourite experiment asked people how much they would be willing to pay for travel insurance that would pay out $100,000 in case of death compared with a policy covering only death by terrorist act. The majority of respondents said they would pay the same, even though death from a terrorist attack is far less likely.[15] Kahneman concludes that this choice (like countless similar decisions) is "irrational" because it deviates from decision-making based on statistical probability. He concludes that algorithm-based systems make better decisions than human experts. On this view, we would be well advised to stop overestimating our competence and admit that our algorithms do a better job.

The astonishing success of Kahneman's ideas with leaders and the general public alike suggests that there are many who see his debunking of our sense of self-importance as a healthy counterweight to a culture that overvalues individual judgement. It plays well among educated elites and the managerial classes who are only too ready to question the wisdom of ordinary people. When this suspicion of human nature is coupled with other popular behavioural economics ideas such as Sunstein and Thaler's (2008) 'nudge' theory, which draws on the same research to propose the use of psychological techniques to manipulate people into healthier and happier lives, we have the makings of another cultural perfect storm.

The problem with the psychological research that behavioural economists like to cite is that in the interests of gathering clean data, 'uncontaminated' by distortions due to human interests, subjectivity or context, it is conducted using methods that exclude from view much of what makes human life meaningful and understandable. Much of the data is based on answers to questionnaires given by individuals in a research setting or mined from large datasets. American public opinion pollster Daniel Yankelovich (1991) has pointed out the fallacies in such research. People do not tell the truth in questionnaires. To complicate things further they each bias their answers for different (and hidden) reasons. We give the answers that we think will make the researcher like us, express our resentment at the inane questions, make us look good to ourselves, and because "it depends" or "I will have to ask my father" are never an option.

Human beings do not live, learn and grow in the kind of relational vacuum that behavioural psychologists set up in these experiments. Human mastery is not simply a collection of competencies the more of which you have, the more competent you are. Nor do we act in situations stripped of relational and cultural contingencies. The fatal flaw in this kind of research is in the unreflective (and in Ariely's words "pessimistic") view of personhood at the centre of its frame. If our decision-making is "irrational", by whose standards of rationality is this judged? If humans are such poor decision-makers, how have we come so far as a species, adapted ourselves to environments from Arctic tundra to tropical rainforests, doubled life expectancy in 100 years, reduced infant mortality, created science and law, built great civilizations and produced great art?

The behaviourist conceptual frame or paradigm – so central to Western thought since the Enlightenment and intensified in the last few decades – permeates the discourse on approaches to enhancing human capacity and in our view has taken us in a dangerously misguided direction.

There Is No Hierarchy of Needs

We would rather return to the spirit enshrined in 1948 and the idea of the 'full development of the human personality'. That would come closer to the original thinking of psychologists like Abraham Maslow – a man whose vision we need to reclaim in these early years of the 21ˢᵗ century.

His thinking has entered the mainstream vernacular in the form of 'Maslow's Hierarchy' – one of the most recognizable of all developmental theories today. It suggests that throughout our lives humans confront a series of needs, each one of a higher order than the last. Once lower level needs are satisfied, development moves to the satisfaction of a higher need, and so on up a pyramid that leads at its pinnacle to the self-actualized individual.

At the base of the pyramid are said to be the most basic physical needs for food, water, sleep. Then come needs for safety, security and shelter. Then social needs, for love, friendship and relationship, and for self-esteem and respect. Finally, at the top of the pyramid, comes the need for 'self-actualization' – meaning, purpose, identity and the desire to make something of one's life.

This notion of human development as a hierarchical progression of stages from lower to higher order needs has become all pervasive, and is almost always associated with Maslow's name.

But Maslow did not in fact see the world like that. First, he emphasized coherence as a fundamental psychological need as great if not greater than the basic material needs for food and shelter. We must be able to make sense of ourselves and our place in the world, otherwise we suffer and we cannot remain in that stage for long. Hence the lure and the comfort of simple stories and reassuring slogans when we find ourselves in over our heads, wrestling with uneasiness. This fundamental need is absent today from almost all popular representations of Maslow's theory.

Yet it is critical – especially in powerful times. Aaron Antonovsky (1996) came to the same conclusion, partly through his study of the concentration camps. His major contribution to the study of health and health promotion was to identify what he called 'a sense of coherence' as critical in determining how we experience stress in practice. If we are confronted with something new and anxiety-inducing, he suggested, how we respond – individually and collectively – will depend on our ability to make sense of the situation "cognitively, instrumentally and emotionally". In other words, do we see the situation as comprehensible – we understand the nature of the challenge; manageable – we believe that the resources to cope with the challenge are available; and meaningful – we are motivated to cope with the challenge and feel that it is worth taking on. If these three sources of coherence are not present then we are more likely to be overwhelmed.

Secondly, Maslow was disappointed by the way his analysis was misinterpreted through the linear mechanistic perspective of modernity and later explicitly retracted this "hierarchy of needs" theory. Detail aside, his principal objection to the trivialization of his ideas was that to him it was self-evident that the 'human personality' is always whole and entire. Our needs are complex, fluid and dynamic and our capacities to address them do not form a hierarchy but in the language of Arthur Koestler (1967), another influence on Maslow, an irreducible "holarchy".

All possibilities are always present. Which will manifest is contingent on experience in the world. At one moment a particular need is salient and must be addressed, at another something else draws our attention and response. Living systems exist in an ever-shifting and exquisitely attuned engagement between our interior lives and the external universe and it is in this engagement that 'being' proceeds.[16]

For Maslow and other humanistic thinkers human maturation is an emergent process achieved uniquely by each individual in their historical confrontation with the existential demands of their own life. It begins with an embodied potential – we are born to become – and unfolds uniquely, in each moment, with each choice. We do not have to satisfy a need for shelter in order to graduate to a need for love. Indeed in the concrete world they cannot be separated. If we are not loved, we will not thrive – to develop self-esteem or anything else.

Certainly one meets the need for love and security in different ways at different stages of life and in different circumstances, but the need and opportunity for personal meaning and fulfilment are always core elements of psychological life. We must make meaning out of our experience that reassures us the world has a knowable order. If we don't we go mad. Even die. As Auschwitz survivor Victor Frankl (1959) has described so powerfully, even in the most degraded circumstances of the Nazi death camps, where all needs were ultimately betrayed, the search for growth and fulfilment did not become subordinated to survival. They reinforced one another. It was Frankl's attempts to find meaning in the relentless horror that enabled him to survive the camp.

Stage models of human development are sometimes useful for naming some of what we notice about competent people. But listing, categorizing and 'staging' what are, in fact, multiply determined capacities is itself a manifestation of an ordered, mechanistic culture that can reduce emergent and holistic phenomena to the status of machinery – the 'ahuman'. Misunderstanding the radical nature of Maslow's proposed new psychology of being, we have projected our own cultural schemas of simple, linear, step-by-step 'hierarchy' on to his comprehensive view of ever-emergent human potential.

Maslow's thinking was neither simple nor conventional and even when he was at his most influential, in the 1950s, he was received with considerable ambivalence by his colleagues. On the one hand he was elected President of the American Psychological

Association in recognition of his leadership in psychological thought. On the other his work was (and still is) rejected by much of academic psychology. When he suggested that human beings must be understood on their own terms not studied through methods developed for investigating the behaviour of billiard balls and fruit flies, he was accused of trying to destroy science.

In his view the paradigm that dominated research at the time was a hold-over from 19th-century natural science and was not up to the task of understanding the complexity of human experience. He and many of his colleagues were urging a new kind of science – a human science – that started from the assumption that humans must be understood holistically as conscious participating beings, agents of their own destiny.

The bias in science against holistic ways of knowing that embrace a wider, more generous and more nuanced view of who we are – our deeper existential questions, moral concerns, solidarity with each other, the capacity for peak experience, love, faith, creativity, and the inexhaustible yearning for meaning – continues.

We remain largely in thrall to the behaviourists who, through their reductionist methods, can more easily assemble quantitative data: the critical currency for today's scientific and policy discourse. Certainly this has its uses. But as Freeman Dyson (2011) pointed out in a review of Daniel Kahneman's book *Thinking, Fast and Slow*, the marriage of the twin gods of our reductionist culture – economics and behaviourism – only makes sense of "our more humdrum cognitive processes":

> *The part of the human personality that Kahneman's method can handle is the non-violent part, concerned with everyday decisions, artificial parlor games, and gambling for small stakes. The violent and passionate manifestations of human nature, concerned with matters of life and death and love and hate and pain and sex, cannot be experimentally controlled and are beyond Kahneman's reach.*

It is clear today that we need to move well beyond the limits of humdrum cognition. Powerful times engage powerful emotions. If we are to develop our 21ˢᵗ-century competencies, manifest our potential as persons of tomorrow, we cannot rely on a science based on reductionist behaviourism. We must also engage the more powerful frame of our irreducible, lived experience.

Defining Competence

Which brings us finally to our chosen definition of 'competence'. In a world beset by definitional struggles we have found support for our own sense of what 'competence' is in the unlikely guise of a five-year, multinational research study by the OECD (2003) to identify "key competencies for a successful life and a well functioning society in the 21ˢᵗ century".

The inquiry was deep and comprehensive, drawing on the best available wisdom from philosophers, sociologists, cognitive scientists and others and including consultations with all OECD countries. It included a rigorous discussion of what we mean by 'competence'.

The editors started by sifting through the lists of possible attributes needed to meet the goal of living a successful life in a well-functioning society. Technical competencies, they acknowledged, are as useful as they have ever been. But they also discovered, echoing Robert Kegan (who participated in the research), that in the operating conditions of the 21ˢᵗ century none of these competencies is of any use, nor can it be developed in practice, unless another level of competence is also present. This is the capacity to handle higher levels of complexity and uncertainty than we are used to. And the only way to tell whether that competence is present is to see it demonstrated in practice.

Hence they arrived at a simple definition of 'competence' in the 21ˢᵗ century, which is also the one we have settled on ourselves:

> *Competence is the ability to meet important challenges in life in a complex world.*

A necessary consequence of this definition is that you cannot measure or assess 21st-century competencies in the abstract. You can only see them as a whole and in action. They can be inferred from successful performance in complex situations in the real world.

The OECD thus ran into a huge methodological problem. They were looking through cultural lenses that attempted to identify specific, isolated competencies such as those listed earlier in this chapter. They were also trying to locate competencies from individual, written assessments of performance in each area, comparable across nations and across cultures. In other words they were trying to assess complex holistic phenomena using reductionist, atomistic and statistical reasoning.

That approach is doomed to failure. Effective action in a complex and pluralistic world is always culturally and context-specific. No 21st-century competence can stand alone. They are all aspects of a single, whole and unique person and are in constant flux and interplay.

The OECD study mournfully concluded that the 21st-century competencies cannot be delivered through our 20th-century structures of measurement, standardization and accountability. That has not stopped people trying to do so – with inevitably disappointing results.

We have taken the opposite approach. Whilst we have researched and analysed numerous lists of 21st-century competencies, and we have no quarrel with them as far as they go, we remain unconvinced that such enumeration will lead us to enlightenment. We rather put our faith in the 'persons of tomorrow' we find in our midst.

In such people we find a cluster of qualities or capacities which in turn underpin the expression of 21st-century competencies; just as one might have an innate capacity for music which can then be expressed as a competence in playing an instrument. The capacity is a quality of the individual, the competence is expressed in action – and can be developed to the point of mastery. It is to this quest that we now turn.

PART TWO:

21ST-CENTURY COMPETENCIES

CHAPTER 4:

ENABLING CONDITIONS FOR 21ST-CENTURY COMPETENCE

Three Literacies: Psychological, Cultural and Epistemic

The first part of this book has outlined the changing global context which calls for us to develop what we have termed '21st-century competencies'. The second half will turn to the question of what those competencies might be and how to develop them in practice.

The following chapters explore that question using a structure first outlined in Jacques Delors' (1996) UNESCO report on education for the 21st century, *Learning: The treasure within.* The report promotes four pillars of learning:

- learning to be
- learning to be together
- learning to know
- learning to do

The structure has been very influential and has become the guiding mantra for a number of education systems around the world (Tawil & Cougoureux, 2013). What most have missed, however, is the critical rider – that we need to develop these capacities in the context of the 21st century as we have described it in part one. That is the focus of the second part of this book.

But there is one prior condition that must be fulfilled, it seems, before people are able to bring these necessary personal qualities to a professional context. It is the critical enabling or 'threshold' competence for the full expression of our potential. This is psychological literacy – the capacity accurately to perceive, recognize, feel and interpret your own and others' psychological experiences as they occur moment by moment and spontaneously to adjust one's behaviour in response to that perception.

We have noted already that the default psychological protection against fear and anxiety is neurotic defence. It is a way of dealing with complexity by withdrawal from contact with the world and so not dealing with it at all.

Persons of tomorrow, by contrast, embrace the world. They engage with their existential reality in a spirit of hope, courage, invention and play. Their engagement is conscious, in the moment, not rule-based or rehearsed. They are participants in events, not victims. They naturally practise what Harold Bridger (1990) called "the double task". They are able to retain the capacity to reflect on their actions even whilst in the midst of them (yet not be paralysed by that awareness – like the athlete who 'chokes' through thinking too much).

This capacity for self-awareness, for poise and grace in action, is widely regarded as the beginning of wisdom and of mastery. This is the first protection against denial as a default response to overwhelm – and thus the pathway to learning and growth.

Given that we are social and spend most our time in small groups, knowing how to read the dynamics of social interplay in the groups in which we operate is another key literacy. Whether running a task team at work, convening a homeowners' group to deliberate on a shared problem or simply hosting a good dinner party, understanding group dynamics and how to facilitate an effective group process makes a difference. Everyone has experienced the frustration of the meeting stymied by one member who can't listen, or one who sits silently until the end and then sabotages what we thought was a group agreement.

Psychological literacy must include today not only an awareness of oneself and our small groups, but also one's cultural context. So much so that we identify 'cultural literacy' as a second critical enabler for 21st century competence.

Cultural literacy is the capacity to perceive, understand and participate fluently in a given culture while knowing there are also other cultures, to be able to meet those other cultures gracefully and respectfully and to transgress cultural norms with conscious subtlety.

Until the modern era in the West, and it is still the case in many of the world's cultures, individuals lived their entire lives within one cultural context. From cradle to grave they were immersed in societies that were deeply coherent. The expectation was that children should be socialized to understand and conform to the givens of life in that society. Those givens covered all that was expected for a successful life.

Today we require a more conscious awareness of culture: an active acknowledgement that we are willy nilly operating inside a cultural context. And more usually today not in one but in many cultures. American school children are required each morning to recite the Pledge of Allegiance, which refers to "one nation, under God, indivisible". Children in the room who are from atheist, Buddhist, pantheist or animist cultures must make a psychological adjustment to feel both part of that one nation, yet not under the same God. Shari, a language teacher in a middle school in Pennsylvania, must teach English to children from 30+ different cultures and languages and she must do it without offending the parents of any of them. The Japanese manager in northern England must understand why his company's group fitness programmes generate resentment and ridicule in the sons and daughters of British coal miners and in turn those same workers must learn to interpret management's actions through a wider cultural frame than the one inherited from their parents.

In the globally connected 21st century every act has cultural significance. Most of us are blind to all but the most obvious. But the person of tomorrow has a subtle cultural awareness, and is at home in a hybrid, shifting, multifarious culture that denies us more traditional sources of stability and identity.

The third important literacy is epistemic literacy (or knowledge literacy if you prefer). Epistemic literacy is the capacity to read the deeper frames underpinning knowledge in any situation, recognizing there are many perspectives on what counts as 'truth' and that we are as likely to see what we believe as believe what we see.

Ubiquitous in the 21st century organizational conversation is the ideal of 'evidence based' decision-making. Increasingly, however, we face the challenge of reconciling different views of what counts as 'evidence'. Whose evidence? Gathered and assembled in what way and by what measures? We need to be aware of how knowledge is created in diverse knowledge landscapes and disciplines – economics, botany, psychology, poetry, politics, gardening – and how difficult it is to weigh any one against the measures of the others. Many of us when asked 'what is the meaning of life?' automatically answer '42'. Douglas Adams's famous joke has penetrated deep into popular culture. It turns precisely on our innate awareness of different ways of knowing which, while complete and reliable in themselves, are fundamentally incommensurable.

Epistemic awareness allows us to recognize these multiple systems of arriving at truth, to make the commitment to our own 'truths' more tentative and therefore open to new knowledge. It reminds us fundamentally that 'objective' knowledge derived from abstraction and reasoning is no more or less valid than 'subjective' knowledge gained from our own unique lived experience.

Competence in Practice

The critical importance of these patterns of awareness, these literacies, was confirmed for us when we decided to explore 21ˢᵗ-century competence in practice. Rather than start constructing the ideal education and training curriculum for the 21ˢᵗ century from multifarious building blocks all around us, instead we decided to look for the finished article, people displaying the competencies we see as essential for the new era, and then find out how they came by them.

We assumed we would find competence in practice in individuals in positions of power and mastery, and so set out to shadow a number of chief executives across a range of sectors – public, private, non-profit – to see what we could learn.

In each case a team of two 'shadows' spent a day with the chief executive, observing how they perform in today's challenging operating environment – and then asking them how they came by their competence. One shadow concentrated on the external environment, the setting. The other, an experienced psychotherapist, focussed on the chief executive's inner world and facility in relationship with others.

The results (qualitative and indicative: this was not intended as a statistically robust survey) were fascinating and surprising. We certainly found confirmation of contemporary stress – physical and psychological. The CEOs we encountered had to cope with long days, little predictability in their lives, disconnection and fragmentation of their teams in a global working environment, and an ever-changing landscape for their operations.

There were some distinctions between the sectors, but these appear more as nuances in a general picture. We found in the private sector a real tension between short-term needs and long-term strategy. Most conversations about time were about adjusting next week's schedule to accommodate new developments, or to conclude conversations or activities that ran beyond the time originally scheduled. Although we were shadowing those in overall charge of the strategic direction of the organization, in practice strategic thinking seemed largely crowded out by other more pressing concerns.

There was also an underlying sadness at the strains on personal loyalty in a fiercely competitive market. Those at the top of their organization have usually devoted their lives to a particular industry, or sector, or even a single company. We could see the personal pain experienced when the final years of 'triumph' coincide with a downturn in the market and the necessity to dismantle what has been built over time, 'letting people go'.

The corporate environment also seemed to leave little room for the full expression of our subjects' humanity. We saw little effort, and perhaps little scope, to stamp a personal identity on office or working space – already heavily branded and cleanly professional. Human interactions like meeting, greeting, serving drinks, making people comfortable, were also often allocated to another, the Personal Assistant – leaving the Chief Executive 'free' to concentrate on the business.

Aping business, we saw some of the same qualities in the public sector too, although branding was less evident and the buildings less obviously designed to impress. Here it was more on the substantive side that we saw limits of expression: chief executives with little executive power. The business day was not a series of strategic conversations and difficult decisions, but rather endless rounds of co-ordination between agencies working in 'partnership', discussions about how to manage scarce resources, and keeping up with a welter of initiatives from central government. We also noticed what long-time government administrator Elsa Porter has described as 'moral loneliness', where the countless moral ambiguities of life in liquid times must be handled – if at all – off stage and in private.

In the non-profit sector we found a generally more flexible and free-wheeling environment. Often these are cause-driven organizations and therefore more likely to be conscious of any disconnect between the cause espoused and the culture of the organization promoting it. Many are also shaped in the image of their founders, giving a more personal and human stamp to the organizational culture. Yet here too there was some of the energy-draining activity of the public sector: complex bureaucratic co-ordination, managing on scarce resources, reacting to policy initiatives. And in some cases, where the organization was modelled in the image of a charismatic founder, succession planning (the requirement for the individual concerned to 'move on') was a clear but undiscussable issue.

As word of our shadowing work spread, a number of arts organizations approached us to be shadowed. We readily agreed. What we found in this sector were some astonishingly impressive individuals, comfortable with themselves and thriving on the complexities and ambiguities of modern life. And although their organizations were in many cases fragile and poorly funded, with no readily identifiable 'business model' to speak of, their work was inspirational – both for audiences and, more importantly for the purposes of our inquiry, for the participants themselves.

We had set out to find 'positive deviants' – people thriving in a world where most of us are struggling. Here they were in abundance.

On reflection, we should not have been surprised. The arts and cultural sector starts at a distinct advantage in helping to grow a culture that nurtures human development, given the (potentially) profound nature of its material. The arts, after all, are essentially in the meaning business. They are all about perception and re-perception, about narrative and sense-making, about human relationship and emotion, about who we are and what we can be, and about questioning and playing with rules rather than blithely following them. These are precisely the qualities we need to enrich if we are to navigate the transition to a more sustainable, effective and fulfilling global culture.

Enabling Conditions

Reflecting on these shadowing encounters and our wider research, we came to a number of significant insights about how to help people grow in practice.

First, the people we encountered and their stories confirmed the truism that lies at the heart of our preferred definition of 'competence'. In other words, 'the ability to meet important challenges in life in a complex world' is learned through the experience of engaging with complex challenges that are motivating and significant for the participants involved. We do not necessarily have to enrol in a special programme, or a school or other institution of learning – so long as the setting we place ourselves in provides challenges of this nature, suited to who we are and who we want to become and we have a trusted guide and mentor at our side for support.

Many of the impressive people we encountered were what the philosopher William James (1907) described as 'twice born'. They had found themselves travelling a particular path, often something quite conventional, and actively chose at some point to shift their career to something more challenging and more meaningful. Developing 21st-century competencies had not been a conscious motivation, but instinctively these people had placed themselves in settings where, so long as they did not sink, they were more likely to learn how to swim in a new way.

Second, it became abundantly clear from studying these individuals through the dual lenses of their inner world and relationships and the external setting in which these play out, that the two are unavoidably symbiotic. In other words, persons of tomorrow are more likely to thrive in 21st-century organizational settings, that is settings that allow them to pause, to reflect, to take on new challenges, to express themselves and to grow.

We had been expecting to find the corporate world of business in the forefront of providing such spaces, given their stated need to attract the best talent and the surveys that show talented people today are on the look-out for places where they can grow and develop.[17] We were disappointed. Rigid structures, particularly when reinforced in response to apparent threats, do not provide these enabling conditions. The creative leaders of the new culture are seeking out more flexible forms – and the two are likely to develop together.

This point is often overlooked. When it comes to competence, and especially to 'leadership', we are still largely in thrall to the cult of the individual. When we point to shining examples of people who have broken free from the gravitational field of the old culture of organizations we usually focus on the character and capacities of the individual rather than see those capacities as inevitably in relationship with the organizations that they build around them and the people within. Leadership and personal development training tend to be focused on taking the individual out of their organizational setting – on 'retreat' – then returning them to impose the new attitudes and behaviours on the workplace.

We work from a different premise. We believe that the potential to express 21st-century competencies is innate and universal. We conclude from the experience of observing high performers in a variety of organizational settings that the setting is critical in determining whether these competencies are evoked and developed or not, particularly the fit between individual capacity and the range of capacities permitted and encouraged.

Finally we found these encounters confirmed the importance of the three literacies – psychological, cultural, epistemic – as key prerequisites for developing 21st-century competencies.

The encounters called to mind Donald Schön's (1983) famous work on what he called the 'reflective practitioner'. Schön's central observation, like ours, is that the changing nature of the challenges posed by the modern world requires us to develop beyond technical expertise. Schön suggests that 'from the perspective of Technical Rationality, professional practice is a process of problem solving. Problems of choice or decision are solved through the selection, from available means, of the one best suited to established ends. But with this emphasis on problem solving, we ignore problem setting, the process by which we define the decision to be made, the ends to be achieved, the means which may be chosen'.

Problem setting is a necessary precondition for technical problem solving, but it is not itself a technical problem. So the reflective practitioner must mix technical rationality with judgement and learning. Rather than simply assuming that following the 'right' method will generate the right result, he or she prefers the approach recommended for adding whisky in a famous recipe for the potent Scottish dessert Athol Brose: 'taste liberally and proceed empirically'.

We noticed in our shadowing encounters that the shadows, even though silent and unobtrusive, were themselves encouraging this more reflective approach in their subject. The CEOs were aware that they were being observed, and so started to become aware of themselves more consciously in the moment. They became more reflective, performing the 'double task' of doing something and reflecting on how they were doing it at the same time. This is the beginning of transformative learning.

We found that the very act of shadowing, not intended as an intervention of any kind, in practice triggered and started to develop this essential, foundational capacity in our subjects. Those familiar with non-directive approaches to counselling will not be surprised: research has shown in that domain that the mere presence of an accepting 'other' creates conditions that nurture the inherent growth process.

The capacity for personal reflection was also matched in the individuals the shadows observed as most competent by the consciousness and intention with which they exercised their competence, and their awareness of how this competence was perceived in different settings. They had a clear sense of the extent to which the culture they found themselves operating in nourished their fullness so that they felt 'at home' or disrespected it or treated it as 'alien'.

We saw, in other words, their cultural literacy and their related capacity as cultural leaders, displaying the cunning and skill necessary to express their 21st-century competencies while in a dominant culture that undervalues them and values its own 'incompetencies' more highly. Even where the organizational setting is generally supportive, that skill might be necessary, for example, to deal with certain departments, or with other organizations, partners, funders and so on where different norms and expectations prevail. Without this level of awareness we find it hard to believe they would have survived and risen to the top of their organizations with the capacities and competencies we saw so evidently intact and embodied.

These shadowing encounters thus helped to ground our inquiry in real, observed performance. They have led directly to the following chapters on how to encourage the expression and development of 21st-century competencies in practice.

CHAPTER 5:

BEING A PERSON OF TOMORROW

Four Pillars of Learning

As noted in the previous chapter, the influential Delors report on learning in the 21st century, *Learning: The treasure within*, outlined a simple structure of four pillars of learning. In order to learn our way into the future, the report concluded, we need to learn how to be, how to be together, how to know and how to do.

We have come to see how these map on to the three literacies explored in the previous chapter. A prerequisite for learning how to be is to become aware of how we are already being, including in relationship with others: psychological literacy.

A prerequisite for learning how to be together is to become aware of how we are already being together in large groups, societies, settled patterns and cultures: cultural literacy.

A prerequisite for learning how to know is to become aware of how we are already knowing, what constitutes knowledge for us and how we respond to knowledge that lies outside our normal frames: epistemic literacy.

We follow the structure of four pillars of learning in the chapters that follow. The first looks at the qualities of being we observe in persons of tomorrow. The next explores how these manifest themselves in large groups and cultures – being together. Then there comes a chapter devoted to exploring how persons of tomorrow make sense of the world, their ways of knowing.

These chapters are mostly about identifying observable qualities and characteristics of the people we see as persons of tomorrow. They are habits of heart and habits of mind. And they are innate in all of us. To an extent their content is interchangeable: who we are inevitably has a big influence on how we work with others and on what and how we know. And vice versa.

The move to 'competence', distinguishing it from these qualities and capacities, is effectiveness in action: 'the ability to meet important challenges in life in a complex world'. Hence the final two chapters dwell on the practicalities of organization and action: learning to do.

It is in action that the person of tomorrow draws on his or her innate qualities and capacities to express and demonstrate 21st-century competencies. And it is in taking on important challenges that demand such competencies that they are developed.

That is the structure of what lies ahead. We turn first to the quality of being.

Being

After two centuries of preoccupation with the idea of a mechanical universe and the image of humans as rational automata performing species-prescribed operations, early in the 20th century those interested in development began to turn their attention to unrealized human potential and to the question of being. William James (1907) wrote that we are "only half awake. Our fires are dampened, our drafts are checked. We are making use of only a small part of our mental and physical potential."

This call to awakening was to become a theme of the popular culture of the mid-20th century as millions became engaged in activities that facilitated self-development. Abraham Maslow's *Towards a Psychology of Being* was a best-seller for years and remains a classic of transformative thought. Maslow and humanistic colleagues agreed with James's expanded view of human potential and set out to build a growth-oriented psychology that put 'being' rather than 'doing' at its centre.

These pioneers of consciousness include Gestalt therapy creator Fritz Perls and Carl Rogers, whose work in encounter groups is featured in the Oscar winning film, *Journey into Self.*

Alan Watts married his Anglican Christian training with mysticism, Taoism and psychedelics. Group psychologist Will Schutz developed the intensive marathon process so popular at the Esalen Institute in California. Romanian Jacob Moreno, a Freudian dissident, introduced 'psychodrama' and put participatory theatre to use as a path to growth. He and Herbert Otto among many others created growth techniques that became the basis for most of the group facilitation methods now used in corporate training worldwide.

Perhaps because we now learn about these human development pioneers principally from their written texts rather than their experiential workshops, often overlooked is the importance of somatic experience in the human potential work of the era. These personal learning processes were not all talk and mindfulness, they reclaimed physical embodiment. Thomas Hanna's 1970's classic *Bodies in Revolt* offered powerful practices to the buttoned down 50s' generation seeking more fully to experience themselves not as 'having' a body but as 'being' a body.

Alongside these developments, interest in the ancient Vedantic and Buddhist methods for deep exploration of multiple states of mind was gaining momentum as a stream of Indian, Japanese and Chinese teachers found ready followers amongst a spiritually hungry generation. Though sometimes side-tracked by pop-gurus who promised a fast track to a New Age, for the vast majority these experiences led to the opening of a wider horizon of awareness and brought a rich menu of pathways to fuller experience of being.

This entire movement towards social and individual transformation was met with scepticism. It was then, and to a large extent remains, a counter-cultural move to pay attention to who and how we are being, rather than just what we are doing, or what we are consuming. So after a flowering of activity within universities, colleges, growth centres and training institutes, by the 1980s being had become marginalized once more.

The idea was resisted by academic behaviourists who saw it as hopelessly subjective and not amenable to the methods of objective inquiry, while the postmodernists and feminists were busy deconstructing notions of inner reality as a hold-over from a Romantic past. So a search for fulfilment that inspired the baby boom generation to awaken to the 'further reaches' of their nature became reduced to an eviscerated, mechanistic 'happiness' science on the one hand, and a superficial postmodernism on the other that denied the reality of any kind of psychological depth.

As the 21st century proceeds, however, and complexity becomes the universal context, the importance of fundamental existential questions intensifies. Precisely because of the pace of change and the rising sense of cultural incoherence that characterizes such transitional times, it is now impossible to leave questions of being out of any holistic consideration of the competencies needed to live well.[18]

In today's environment – fast-moving, confusing, full of surprises – persons of tomorrow typically display a cluster of qualities of being that set them aside from the crowd. We outline them below under three headings: humility, balance and faith in the future. When we encounter such people we sense these qualities. If we develop them in our own way of being then we are more likely to be able to express the 21st-century competencies within us.

Humility

The essential quality of today's complex world is its sheer unknowability. It is incalculable. Every advance in knowledge reveals new areas of ignorance. The number of possible interconnections even in a simple system soon becomes too great for the fastest computer processor to handle. Identification of 'the system in question' itself is highly selective, and requires ignoring the 99% of the universe that constitutes 'the system not in question'.

The person of tomorrow is comfortable acknowledging what Don Michael (1972a) called "the fact of our ignorance" – that we really don't know what we are talking about much of the time. We are finite, vulnerable human beings, however much we seek to hide the fact from others and from ourselves through elaborate defensive routines. Those defences close down ways in which we can be more present, consciously participating in the world as an open system.

The former US commander in chief in Afghanistan, General Stanley McChrystal (2009)[19], is an unlikely standard bearer for this quality. His initial 66-page assessment report to President Obama on the state of the war in Afghanistan is a masterpiece on the intricate realities of modern policy-making:

> *What we face is a uniquely complex environment, where there are at least three regional and resilient insurgencies, with further sub-insurgencies. They have intersected on top of a dynamic blend of local power struggles in a country damaged by 30 years of war.*
>
> *Where you build the well, what military operations to run, who you talk to: everything that you do is part of a complex system with expected and unexpected, desired and undesired outcomes, and outcomes that you never find out about. In my experience, I have found that the best answers and approaches may be counterintuitive; the opposite of what it seems like you ought to do is what ought to be done. When I am asked what approach we should take in Afghanistan, I say 'humility'.*

Humility does not come easily for people brought up on bullet points and clear answers. True, there is a growing recognition of humility as the critical enabler of relationship, openness and trust (in Ed and Peter Schein's *Humble Leadership*) or as a valuable human advantage in the machine age (Edward Hess and Katherine Ludwig's *Humility is the New Smart*). Yet it remains the case that for Americans in particular, who have raised pride and self-esteem to a high art, even the word 'humility' raises hackles. It is more acceptable – even expected – for Americans to sing their own praises. When Mohammad Ali was taken to task, chided for arrogance when he claimed he was "the greatest", he said "It ain't arrogant if you can do it!" Fifty years later, young Americans are still told this story by their sports coaches as they are encouraged to succeed. Maybe for winning at sports it's not bad advice, but as a preparation for life in the messy uncertainties of the 21st century it has all the hallmarks of a neurotic response.

To be clear: adopting this stance of humility does not mean giving up on understanding or on the need to take action (with both too much and too little information). We are learning all the time more about coordination dynamics, complexity and emergence, which are giving us fresh ways to think about complex systems. Central to these approaches is an understanding of emergence, in which new types of order appear that are not predictable, or even explainable after the event, by reference to individual system components. For the world described by the new science of complexity we will need to develop an attitude of humility as a prerequisite for learning.

That is the way of the master: to be in the world as a learner in turn encourages and catalyses learning in others. Persons of tomorrow naturally provide space for others to grow into, rather than fill it with their own knowing. They share their problems and questions as a gateway to mutual learning, rather than their answers and successes as an invitation to praise. They have their egos under control and fill the airspace with their listening.

This too is counter-cultural. The gift of modernity was to advance a way of thinking that focused on individual sovereignty, liberty, dignity and creativity. That has led, in some views, to a narcissistic overshoot, particularly in the Anglo-Saxon dominated cultures, culminating in the 20th century, the 'century of the self', in which relationships have become merely an extension of individual choices. So Bellah *et al.* (1985) in their critique of the excesses of American individualism caution that where families and relationships are based on individualistic utilitarianism and marriages either on a negotiated contract between self-interested individuals or on romantic expressive individualism (where authentic self-expression brings the couple together), the basic principle is the same. "No binding obligations and no wider social understanding justify a relationship. It exists only as the expression of free selves who make it up." And if it no longer meets the needs of either individual, it ends.

By contrast, persons of tomorrow, though fully alive as individuals, are also at home in their relationships. Capacities such as loyalty, partnership, friendship, altruism, empathy, solidarity, support, nurturance and followership, are necessary ingredients for thriving in the 21ˢᵗ century.

This same lack of narcissism means that persons of tomorrow are fully and recognizably human. Against the cult of the superhero, they are obviously just regular people without airs or graces. They follow in the long line of sages 'sweeping the temple floor'. They self-evidently enjoy the fulfilments of a human life – laughing, loving, living, appreciating beauty, feeding the senses. Ruth Little (2011), the Australian dramaturg and Literary Manager of the Royal Court Theatre in London (herself a person of tomorrow), reminds us that the Latin root of 'humility' is humus, meaning ground. Persons of tomorrow are grounded, living and working *in* the world.

Compassion arises naturally as a close relative of this humble sense of self. In most of the world's religions, the capacity to be with another in their suffering without judging and in solidarity holds a pre-eminent place. If others are to share their own challenges, their vulnerabilities, their growing edge rather than their mastery or established power, then they need to sense a space in which they will be treated with dignity and compassion.

Persons of tomorrow provide such a space – and it starts with themselves. For it requires a certain generosity towards oneself to admit to less than mastery and to give way to others to let them flourish in one's presence. And it takes courage not to turn away from one's fear, uncertainty and even suffering. It requires strength and confidence – but is not commonly perceived in that way.

The root of courage is the Latin 'cor' – it is a quality of heart. Persons of tomorrow are typically big-hearted. That allows them to make the first move where more timid souls may hold back. They are participants rather than bystanders – throwing themselves into learning from experience. They engage rather than shrink into the background, and are in consequence often open and engaging characters in themselves.

This quality of heart is also evident in their stamina, energy and capacity to endure. Like most of us in today's busy, striving, anxious world, persons of tomorrow work hard. That requires them to look after themselves and marshal their energies. And since for the most part their work is against the grain of the dominant culture, it also requires a particular fierceness and determination, psychological strength and stamina. Denial and disinterest are always easier and tempting alternatives to persevering against resistance.

It is an anatomical fact that the heart feeds itself first. It takes the oxygen it needs to keep functioning before pumping that same life force around the body. Persons of tomorrow are not martyrs who neglect their own wellbeing while they look out for others. They include themselves among the people they care for. They are often catalysts for remarkable projects and inspirational activity: but the catalyst has failed if it burns up in the experiment.

Balance

Burning up in the experiment is a real concern. Our shadowing experience revealed the dangers of operating at the leading edge of a culture that finds it difficult to support and appreciate the 21st-century competencies. Stress, burn out, overwork and the common means by which we self-medicate for these conditions (caffeine, alcohol, obsessive fitness training, etc) seem endemic and to be getting worse. Hence another critical quality in the person of tomorrow: balance.

Aristotle wrote in his *Nicomachean Ethics* that "virtue must have the quality of aiming at the intermediate". He identified courage, for example, as just such a midpoint between cowardice at one extreme and recklessness at the other. The person of tomorrow is courageous in this sense: judicious, conscious, grounded, balanced.

Balance is clearly significant. All of the metaphors for today's operating environment suggest the difficulty of keeping one's feet: shifting sands, liquid modernity, waves of change, white water, perfect storms. On one level the balance required is metaphorical – speaking to a quality of mind where emotions and reason are weighed in the course of choosing an action. But there are many traditions of personal growth and self-mastery in which balance, poise and grace are nurtured as real physical capacities.

Our over-intellectualized modern culture has tended to forget connections between mind and body. We are nevertheless more likely to believe what we feel as a physical experience than what we think. And when we are in danger, or under pressure, or anxious, we often experience what Daniel Goleman calls an "amygdala hijack" where suddenly our emotions tend to crowd out rational thought. That's why fighter pilots, for example, have such intensive training – so that the right thing to do becomes instinctive when the body is suffused with fear. As one instructor puts it: "when you climb inside the cockpit your IQ rolls back to that of an ape".

But we can learn to maintain our equilibrium, even when under threat. The way of the warrior, or the martial artist, throughout the ages has been both a physical and a spiritual discipline: developed over time in order to maintain full capacity, in the moment, whatever the circumstances. Many persons of tomorrow turn out to pursue some kind of mindfulness practice or discipline, and keep themselves in good physical shape. They are aware of their bodies. They are in control of their emotions – able to vary their range at will, and to maintain an even temper. They typically display grace under pressure, a quality that brings out the best in others.

We also often see a particular pattern of experience. Persons of tomorrow have often experienced and become socialized in more than one culture – they are boundary spanners with 'hybrid' personalities. They can adapt their language and bearing to circumstance, like tuning forks that find a point of resonance.

Faith in the Future

It might seem a truism to suggest that persons of tomorrow have their eyes on the future. But it is surprising how rare a quality this is. Throughout this book we have put an emphasis on development and growth in response to a fast-changing environment. But that is not a given. Our first response to change is often defensive: to deny the shift in the environment and seek to prop up the status quo. When fissures appear we fill the potholes, rather than digging up the foundations and building anew.

That is particularly true, paradoxically, in times of radical change. Because it is in those moments, when the pillars of the established order are most obviously listing, that we feel most fearful about what is to come. Zygmunt Bauman (2010) talks of living in the 'inter-regnum', when the old rules are discredited but the new order has yet to emerge. If the lineaments of the new order were clear it would be much easier to look forward. Like the flying trapeze artist, we would be more ready to let go our hold if we could see the next trapeze swinging into view.

Even in a transitional era of shifting norms and perceptions, persons of tomorrow are oriented firmly towards transformation. They are able to name the neurotic tendency to fix and cling to systems past their sell-by date. They resist the tendency themselves. They operate in a context of their own making, which embraces a vision of systems, practices, worlds transformed – a vision that inspires both themselves and those around them. And they are able to identify and increase aspects of practice in the present that feed that vision, and give hope to others that it is not idle fantasy.

They are architects of 'next practice', alive to the myriad promptings of a changing environment, both threats and opportunities. Their work is clearly informed by a future consciousness, not a nostalgic desire for restoration of an imagined past. As Shakespeare's Brutus says: "There is a tide in the affairs of men which, taken at the flood, leads on to fortune." Persons of tomorrow, like the surfers out in the bay, lie in wait for that tide, reading the landscape, ready to turn it to their transformative purpose with timely and wise (future-facing) initiative.

Their way of being and acting in the world is therefore aspirational. 'Sustainability', 'resilience' and other fashionable concepts are gaining traction in our quest for longer-term, more responsible thinking. But persons of tomorrow are not content with longevity, or robustness, or mere survival as a goal. They ask 'sustainability for what?', 'for what purpose?'.

They operate from within a strong moral framework. They are concerned with responding to human suffering and realizing human potential. They look for the human in any situation, even in cases of utter devastation, and seek to build relationships from any small seed that will grow and pattern lives and culture anew in ways that are restorative of – and feed – life. They have a faith in the future and in human nature. Just as Carl Rogers' person-centred approach assumed that, given the right supportive environment, sooner or later a new pattern of coherence will emerge out of confusion and conflict. That same faith is evident in Martin Luther King Jr's conviction that "the arc of the moral universe is long but it bends towards justice" – a line that Barack Obama had embroidered on a rug in the White House.

In other words, they hold open the possibility of hope. Not optimism – which like pessimism rests on an assumption that we have no control over the future – but hope. The future is radically open, and it is shaped by who we choose to be in the present. Persons of tomorrow are remarkably patient and resilient: they are not waiting to achieve a vision, they are living it already.

What persons of tomorrow seek to sustain, embody and practice in action is human aspiration – the constant striving for something better. They are relatively less fearful therefore of disruption, discontinuity or even collapse, seeing them as inevitable parts of the life cycle of transformation. It may be that "Things fall apart; the centre cannot hold": persons of tomorrow provide a new, catalytic centre, a hopeful and spacious centre, the crucible of future viability for the world of tomorrow.

CHAPTER 6:

CULTURAL LEADERSHIP AND THE PERSON OF TOMORROW

Being Together

The second pillar is learning to 'be together' – in other words, the capacity to be in relationship with others, to operate in groups. Persons of tomorrow do not forget that they are persons and that whatever else they do they operate in a human system. Importantly, they recognize the other participants in the system are as human as they are. And as the great systems theorist Sir Geoffrey Vickers (1983) said, "human systems are different".

From birth on, as conscious agents located in particular bodies, participating in particular relationships, in a particular place and time, we engage the world as we find it – in middle class Mumbai, a rural African village or central Paris; in a large family or as a single parent; whether our surroundings are violent, supportive, high stimulation or low. There is an infinite variety of contexts for life. As the child learns and the adult goes about life, circumstances offer some options but not others. And when a choice is made, other options are not taken. At the centre of it all, making choices and making meaning, is a unique and sovereign person constructing his or her life as best they can from the opportunities at hand. Nobody else can do it for them. And every life is unique.

It might be the case that the unique experience and inner reality of living our own lives is so special as to leave us incomprehensible to others. That is certainly what psychoanalysts and existentialists have believed. In their view the gap between individual human beings is unbridgeable and, despite our deep longing to connect with others, condemns us to walk through the world alone.

But the Freudians and existentialists, faithful sons and daughters of the Enlightenment, had it wrong. Overly enamoured of the amazing cognitive capacities of the ego and suspicious of religious ecstasy and mob rule, they were forgetting about the capacity – developed in mammals at least since we nurtured offspring with milk and cuddles – for empathy.

In recent years the individualism at the centre of much 20th-century psychology has come under challenge from several directions. One source has been developmental researchers who noted that the organizing principle of women's development was not individual autonomy but relational fulfilment and freedom to act within relationships. Another source is the observations of non-Western psychologists who point out that people of Asian and of tribal heritage find the prospect of psychological autonomy arid and unappealing.

Perhaps even stronger evidence of our fundamental connectedness is the work of a group of neuroscientists at the University of Parma in Italy who discovered mirror neurons in monkeys – circuits in one monkey's brain that fire spontaneously in sympathy when the same cluster of neurons fire in the brain of another monkey.

Mirror neurons have now been found in humans where their function is even more complex. In humans, if the subject even imagines that another person is about to do something, mirror neurons will fire in anticipation. Ramachandran (2011) likes to call these structures the "Gandhi neurons" because, he says, "they blur the boundary between self and others". They allow us to put ourselves in the shoes of the other not only as an intellectual exercise but as a felt embodied experience that goes on without our volition. When someone is in pain, we feel the pain too; likewise when they feel happiness or joy.[20]

Sovereignty then becomes a matter of living in the nexus of these multiple inputs, interpretations and actions artfully enough to take effective action. Sovereignty and individuality do not condemn us to aloneness. They provide us with a unique vantage point from which to know and explore the world. But to know more fully we need to know ourselves and the world through our bonds with each other.

All cultures count on it. It is through our inherent capacity to know others in an immediate way and to be aware of the collective impact we have on each other through language and culture that we come to understand our shared destiny. And with this growing awareness of our fundamental connectedness comes the possibility of growing beyond the ego- and ethno-centricism of youth and achieving the mature capacity for compassion, the mainstay of all spiritual traditions.

The Enlightenment in the 18th century anointed objective reason as the capacity that would banish ignorance and gain us mastery over the universe. But that dream has run its course. If our reading of the historical landscape presented here is valid, in a communion of morally situated subjects rather than a collection of morally neutral objects, a human system, we must privilege the quality of empathy: the ability to walk in another's shoes, to listen to another as if to oneself, to recognize an ethic of interconnectedness, to accept a common ground of being in humanity and love. These are qualities of persons of tomorrow. We must be able to operate well in relationship with others.

This is doubly important given that a growing number of studies suggest that the context of our contemporary lives is making us less empathic. In one study tracking the empathy of young people as they enter university, researcher Sara Konrath found that they score 40% lower on empathy than students did in the 1970s. The decline has become faster since 2000. Konrath (2011) speculates that the cause of this acceleration is social media, which exploded into the lives of young people about then. She and others looking at changing psychological capacities in the 21st century raise an alarm that the conditions of our times might be deadening the capacity for fellow feeling. Persons of tomorrow must deliberately cultivate it.

The Importance of Culture

This follows from the fact that the person and the setting they are in develop in parallel. In order to flourish in the longer term, persons of tomorrow need to help bring about at a collective, human system level what we might call the 'culture of tomorrow'. By developing the qualities that allow them to express their 21st-century competencies in an empathic fashion they will help to evoke the same expression in others, and in so doing are sowing the seeds of a new culture.

Culture matters. We have become used to discussing competencies as skills or qualities exhibited by individuals. That is the Western way, deeply ingrained in our systems of education, training and evaluation. But studies of the differences between how people in diverse cultures see and process their worlds reveal that culture and competence exist as functions of each other.

At one level culture literally determines what we see. In the past decade researchers across the globe have been accumulating evidence showing that many aspects of mental functioning differ in people raised in different cultural contexts. Culture-related differences have been identified for attention; what we actually see; what motivates us to strive; how meaning is construed; neurological development and emotional responses that get triggered by experience; what and how we learn; how we know what we know; and so on.

The significance of this body of research cannot be over-estimated. It emphasizes the critical impact of culture on who we are, even down to the level of what we see when we look out on what we take to be a singular, physical 'reality' and also how we feel about it.

Culture also conditions what we perceive as competence. In the early days of the European colonization of North America, several colleges were established to educate native youth – among them Harvard, Dartmouth and the College of William and Mary. Indigenous American leaders, however, were less than enthusiastic about these schools. Many declined the invitation to send their children to college because, in the opinion of tribal leaders, boys who had previously gone to be educated in the white man's schools had returned to the tribe "ruined" and good for nothing.

Although taught to read, write and calculate, they had not learned culturally important knowledge such as how to hunt or skin a deer, they had no leadership skills, and they knew almost nothing of the ways of the ancestors. In the chiefs' view these products of European education were not real men and were unfit for life in the real world. As a result, many chiefs responded by sending the children of their enemies instead (McLuhan, 1972).

Competence and culture must be considered together, as two sides of the same coin. As the Onondaga chiefs knew, what is competent in one culture may be a liability in another. In more stable times one solution, as Maria was counselled by her girl friends in West Side Story, was to "stick to your own kind". What has changed is that the person of tomorrow cannot choose to live in one culture or another: the culture of the early decades of the 21st century is hybrid, liquid, global.

Cultural Literacy

The place where we typically encounter 'culture' in practice today is at the level of the group, the team, the community, the organization. As we move from setting to setting we are conscious of the often subtle shifts in culture and group dynamics that are in play.

The interest in understanding these group dynamics has tended to shift in recent years towards the virtual world of social networking, online communities, 'tribes' and the like. But there is also a body of older knowledge that can help us become better able to 'read' groups and cultures 'in the flesh' and thus become more effective in shifting the culture in group settings.

We think of the seminal work of social psychologist Kurt Lewin and Wilfred Bion, for example, who developed a psychoanalytic view advanced at the Tavistock Institute in London. Or existentialist psychiatrist Irving Yalom and Bruce Tuckman, whose 'forming, storming, norming, performing' rubric is known to everyone who ever facilitated a group.

Carl Rogers came to see the balance between self-assertion and self-transcendence as critical, both in individuals and in groups. It is a distinction derived from Arthur Koestler's work on 'holons' – the Janus-faced entities that contain both a capacity to participate in the integrity of the whole and to assert their individual identity against or within that whole. Aspects of an entity that express wholeness and integration are 'self-transcendent' and those that express identity and agency are 'self-assertive'. These descriptions apply to individual persons and to the entities they create together – families, groups, organizations, clans, even whole societies.

Persons of tomorrow have mastered this Janus state. They experience themselves as autonomous, aware and self-assertive individuals with a clear sense of agency and identity and at the same time have developed the skills and the willingness to participate and to align themselves to the purposes of some larger whole. In Koestler's view these descriptions apply to individual persons and to the entities they create together – families, groups, organizations, clans, even whole societies.

Though never as neat as Koestler's categories suggest, it is possible and hopefully useful to identify different organizational constellations based on them. A group, for example, may be made up of self-assertive individuals with a clear individualistic sense of self and the group itself also have clear sense of itself as 'us' and not 'them'. Alternatively, self-assertive individuals might form a group that is itself self-transcendent, concerned with some purpose beyond itself. It is also possible for a group to be made up of members who are in a self-transcendent state while the group itself is self-assertive. Finally, a group may be made up of members in a self-transcendent state where the group also has a sense of purpose beyond itself and permeable boundaries with regard to its environment. All of these constellations have strengths and weaknesses and offer different trade-offs for group members between individual freedom and the security of belonging.

In Western societies we are more familiar with the pattern of self-assertive individuals in a self-assertive group. In the typical liberal democratic nation-state, unencumbered, self-assertive sovereign citizens are free to take principled action within a self-assertive collective (the family, nation, institution, political party). The collective asserts its power to act on the world. In families this set up produces a dynamic common in Caucasian middle-class America where children and parents are encouraged to express their individual independence and autonomy but when operating as a whole family they are a clearly recognizable unit – the Joneses – who assertively press their particular interests. It is the kind of culture nurtured by global brands keen to press a coherent brand message and 'brand values' across many different cultures. Politically aligned think tanks fit into this form, where intellectual freedom is exercised in the interests of a particular agenda. We see it too in identity politics and single-issue NGOs, again promoting a single view, a single message, across the world with force and assertiveness.

Alternatively, self-assertive individuals, agents free to act, may choose to do so within a culture that recognises its contribution to a larger whole and seeks to partner and collaborate rather than dominate or impose. Participants in this pattern of group culture might be effective community leaders, global citizens, organisers of alliances, networks of NGOs, or dynamic social entrepreneurs. At their best, universities fit into this cultural constellation, where individual researchers, protected by academic freedom, express their own particular views and are encouraged to take even heretical positions in the service of a transcendent goal – a collegial search for truth and the broader good of society. This type of organization is typical of the 'network' where loosely coupled communities emerge made up of creative, self-assertive individuals working together for a greater good.

When a self-transcendent individual finds him or herself in a group that asserts itself in the world a different dynamic occurs. This combination creates a culture where people find their sense of self not as an individual ego but through participation in a larger group identity. It is likely that this constellation represents the oldest and most enduring relationship between the individual and the group. At its best such a group provides a setting where people join forces with others related by kinship or who are like-minded and are then able to collaborate on larger projects than might have been possible acting individually. Many of the world's religions express this type of organization. Individuals dedicate their lives to a greater cause – sometimes God, sometimes the Church, sometimes the work. Institutions such as the military, political ideologies and sports teams operate in this way, encouraging the sacrifice of individual personhood in exchange for belonging to the larger group and sharing in its higher purpose.

This type of group is both very strong when everyone is aligned, and very vulnerable to disruption by rapid change, innovation or heresy. This is the territory of martyrdom, group solidarity, identity politics, bureaucracy, organised labour, companies with strong corporate cultures, and fundamentalist groups. Individuals surrender their separate identity to participate in the formation of a cohesive group identity which is itself assertive about its purposes, rights and place in the world.

Finally, we can find groups made up of individuals in a self-transcendent state within a group that also seeks to participate in a wider context. In this state there can emerge what Renée Levi (2003) describes as "group magic" where a deep resonance is experienced between the members of the group, the group itself and the emerging context in which the group exists.

In our work we reserve the term "wise groups" for this state where people are fully present and accepted as themselves – free to express their uniqueness, even their quirkiness – but in ways that are exquisitely attuned to a deeper shared flow that moves everyone towards becoming. In our experience this state is always an achievement, arrived at through the stages of group development described by Tuckman and adding a transcendent perspective. Key to this is trust – trust in each other, trust in the purpose of the group and trust in some larger reality of which the group is a part. In wise groups people are aware of themselves as sovereign centres of creativity but they experience this within a larger collective consciousness that itself is part of larger wholes. Such groups seem to produce more than their fair share of extraordinary performance.

This is the domain of transformative cultural leadership. If a collapsing culture cannot access this space it is doomed to fail.

Navigating the Cultural Landscape

Bearing these dimensions of self-assertiveness and self-transcendence in mind, we may begin to chart the collective and cultural territory that persons of tomorrow need to be able to inhabit in today's fluid circumstances.

In the USA in the mid-20th century, a person would be fine in the typical liberal, nation-state culture – a self-assertive individual in a self-assertive group. There need be no cognitive dissonance between how a person might see him or herself as an individual and how the dominant culture wants them to be.

But over the past fifty years a gradual shift has occurred. The modal psychology today is moving towards self-transcendence and collaboration. Nations, even powerful ones, have no guarantees that their power will prevail. Collaboration across boundaries is necessary to maintain stability within and among groups.

The 20th century, the bloodiest in human history, brought humanity to the brink of nuclear planetary suicide debunking perhaps forever the idea that might makes right. In 1957 the Treaty of Rome established a European Community between nations that just a decade before had been at war with each other. Nations that for centuries had been enemies and had tried to impose their dominion over others through acts of imperial self-assertiveness made a shift in the direction of self-transcendence to forge collaborative alliances.

It is true that the fragility of this shift has become apparent in recent years with the rise of nationalism across the world and the divisiveness of the political discourse. As collective anxiety rises, the trust necessary for maintaining a self-transcendent stance for any length of time gets harder to come by. It is tempting to interpret the fractiousness of the current global situation as a return to more self-assertive group consciousness, but we believe that would be wrong.

After all, though Donald Trump became the US president in 2016 by appealing to nationalism and xenophobia, he did not in practice win the popular vote and there remains significant, active and vocal support for the Obama-era shift towards inclusion, trust and connection. Likewise, the travails of the UK in attempting to leave the European Union have if anything strengthened solidarity within the remaining 27 nations and have led in the UK to some of the largest pro-EU demonstrations anywhere on the continent.

Meanwhile, pursuing a business as much as a geopolitical logic, corporations are today making a similar cultural shift towards operating through partnerships and distributed networks. They are finding that the capacities needed to lead within multi-stakeholder networks of systems within systems that characterise life in the liquid present are of a different order from those needed in simpler times.

Cultural leaders today must have a highly developed sense of group dynamics and group potential within this shifting landscape. They must know how to wait for and seek to prompt those magic group moments when there is resonance among members. Levi describes this as "a felt sense of energy, rhythm or intuitive knowing occurring in a group of human beings that positively influences the way they interact towards a common purpose".

These synergies of collective action are well known for sports teams, for groups in acute crisis and for high-performing groups of musicians or actors. When members can achieve a state where they become attuned to each other and to the purposes of the whole, a group can play well above its weight. There is an almost uncanny level of expanded knowledge available to them and they find they can handle complex and ill-defined problems beyond the capacity of any of the individual members. This is the prize of moving to the culture of self-transcendence and collaboration – and it is one we can ill afford to squander.

We do not talk much about this in the West with our preference for individualism, intellectual engagement and rationality. Outside particular settings such as mystical sects or some religious traditions we have no positive language for collective consciousness that only becomes manifest as an emergent process of groups. We are scared of ecstatic surrender, we talk nervously of 'mob rule', and warn about the dangers of group think and suicide cults. We can be wary of being carried away.

But our research suggests that when people can loosen their ego boundaries and give over (and we mean give as in 'gift', not give as in 'hand over') their own individualized subjectivity to fully participate in a collective subjectivity, sometimes remarkable powers become possible. Part of what we need to learn as a species is how to access those states without being afraid of them, and how to spot those who might exploit them for destructive purposes.

Cultural Leadership

All of which brings us to emphasize the role of persons of tomorrow in cultivating the capacity for conscious cultural leadership. Our challenge is not only to develop individuals capable of thriving in the complex world of the 21st century. We also need to develop leaders who are able to shift the culture in which we all live in directions supportive of the qualities already elaborated – humility, balance, aspiration, empathy, reflection and so on.

If the culture is not supportive of these qualities then, by default, it is supportive of – and will continue to develop and to privilege – others. It is not uncommon for individuals to outgrow a position or an organization and feel the need to move on. In cultural terms, we have seen time and again people who are developing 21st-century competencies starting to feel unfulfilled or undervalued in the 20th- century organizational cultures where they are working.

But if humanity is going to navigate successfully the years of turbulence it finds itself in, then those 20th-century organizations must themselves develop. Hence the importance of 'riding two paradigms': it is a critical 21st-century competence to have the subtlety, the cunning, the vision to deploy and express these new competencies in self and in others inside an initially unpromising context. This is cultural leadership – consciously seeking to encourage the culture around us to evolve.

The old testament scholar Walter Brueggemann (2001) likens this challenge to the role of the prophet. The task is threefold: to warn about the dangers and iniquities of the existing system; to paint a desirable vision of the promised land; and to maintain energy and commitment in the people during the 40 years in the wilderness it will take to make the transition.

In his book *Radical Hope: Ethics in the face of cultural devastation,* the philosopher Jonathan Lear tells the story of one such prophet and cultural leader, Plenty Coups, chief of the Crow nation at the end of the 19th century. His tribe were coming under pressure from the white man to give up their way of life and enter the reservation. The culture that had supported and defined the Crow nation's world was threatened with collapse.

Plenty Coups described the transition many years later as follows: "When the buffalo went away the hearts of my people fell to the ground, and they could not lift them up again." As one Crow woman put it, in terms that many would echo today: "I am trying to live a life I do not understand."

Some tribes gave in to despair, accepted the myth of the white man's 'superiority' and the inevitable loss of their culture. Resistance was futile. Some – like Sitting Bull and the Sioux –

chose to go down fighting. To the bitter end, as it turned out. Neither was successful in negotiating a cultural transition.

But Plenty Coups had a dream that although the buffalo would vanish, provided they kept attuned to changing conditions the Crow would come through to find a new way of living. Lear calls this 'radical hope' – the hope for cultural rebirth, but without any predetermined vision of what that rebirth will look like. In the event Crow youth learned the white man's law, negotiated favourable settlements, maintained far more of their land than any other tribe and came to reinvent notions of honour and courage in a world without warriors. Lear writes:

> *There may be various forms of ethical criticism that*
> *one might be tempted to level at this form of*
> *hopefulness, that it was too complacent; that it*
> *didn't face up to the evil that was being inflicted on*
> *the Crow tribe. But it is beyond question that the*
> *hope was a remarkable human accomplishment – in*
> *no small part because it avoided despair.*

This is a story for our times. As the skies turn dark and the 'imminent collapse of civilization' literature grows, if we are to avoid the predictable future of collapse we too are in need of inspiration. Plenty Coups was skilfully riding two paradigms, using the cultural weight of his dream (revered in the existing culture) as a bridge. The true cultural leader is able not only to paint a picture of a better future (anyone can do that) but to embody that and make it relevant in the present.

Changing Cultures

Cultures – even small-scale cultures – change slowly, organically. They are always in motion, always in transition – what anthropologist Grant McCracken (2008) refers to as "culture by commotion".[69] You cannot just replace one culture with another.

But cultures do shift over time, and according to a familiar pattern. There is always a dominant culture side by side with practices that challenge the norms of that way of life. Cultures evolve as examples of new practice are nurtured, in the soil of the old culture but not in support of it.

The beginning of successful cultural leadership is therefore always a small act of creative transgression. It is small because transgression on a larger scale amounts to revolution and will be vigorously resisted. And because the smaller – and cheaper – it is, the easier it is for others to follow the lead.

It must also be transgressive because in order to shift the culture we must challenge it: we must do something counter-cultural. And it is creative, rather than merely disruptive, because it appeals to the culture's deeper values, its 'better self'.

Luiz Eduardo Soares, for example, an anthropologist, philosopher and political scientist appointed Director of Public Safety in Rio de Janeiro in 1999, wanted to reduce the murder rate amongst young men, particularly the number of police involved in committing the murders. He knew he needed to shift the culture in the police force. So he introduced the 'cool police station' programme to make civil police stations more welcoming, human and professional. He put flowers on the front desks and hired university students to act as receptionists. He started to bring more women into the force. Slowly the culture began to shift. It was not these small creative transgressions that led to his downfall, but his more overtly revolutionary public attacks on corruption at senior levels. He was forced out of office after just over a year.

To take a very different example, from early 2008 artist Luke Jerram started placing battered old street pianos in anonymous public places for anyone to play. He installed nearly 100 pianos in towns and cities across the UK, and now cities all over the world are following his lead. He has struggled everywhere with local council regulations, health and safety, and in London had to apply for an individual music licence for each piano (a matter subsequently raised in the House of Lords). But wherever it goes Jerram's 'Play Me I'm Yours' project has transformed community and relationship and lit up people's lives.

Or consider the introduction of IFF's Kitbag into schools

and other group settings. This is a very simple set of resources designed to encourage and support a robust culture of mutual support and respect in any group. There is calming oil for the pulse points, mindfulness and breathing exercises to reconnect participants with themselves, a talking stick to encourage generous and respectful listening, a set of animal cards each representing some innate and valuable human quality that can be prompted in participants and in the group as a whole through their use – joy, grace, power, love. Kitbag has taken off in schools where children, given these and other simple prompts, naturally fall into a culture of kindness, empathy and self-reflection. They then draw their teachers, their family members and carers into this same cultural pattern. And it turns out these simple resources work as well in the Boardroom as they do in the classroom – supporting psychological literacy at the level of the organization.

These interventions are subtle, small scale, low or no cost. But in the economy of meaning they are highly significant – and have been recognized as such. Think of Rosa Parks's refusal to give up her seat on a bus in Alabama (Shipp, 2005). They evoke a collective social resource that lies hidden in a dominant culture under strain. Cultural leadership is always evocative rather than instrumental.

Ultimately its effectiveness relies on a paradox. In order to transgress within a culture you must first be accepted into it. And for the culture to evolve, the transgression must at some level be welcomed and permitted. Thus Gandhi's philosophy of non-violent protest relied on the British reluctance to attack those who do not fight. It was an appeal to the British administrators' better nature.

This is a dynamic beautifully captured by Aftab Omer (2005). He suggests that in times of stability the centre of a culture is conventional – dense with rules, norms, taboos – while the periphery is marginalized, even scapegoated.

During periods of dynamic change, however, like today, the centre becomes more receptive to the different and the unknown:

> *Cultural leaders choreograph this interaction in ways
> that are creative and transformative. In this way
> cultural leadership is distinct from political and
> administrative leadership. While political leaders
> primarily make rules and administrative leaders
> primarily enforce rules, cultural leaders like Gandhi,
> Martin Luther King, and Mother Theresa find
> principled and imaginative ways to transgress those
> rules that inhibit the emergence of cultural
> sovereignty and creativity. Their actions engender
> new and unexpected meanings. The recognition and
> creative transgression of rules and norms is at the
> heart of cultural leadership... Cultural leaders are
> able to transmute how they are personally affected by
> the culture into creative action that midwives the
> future.*

At its highest level, such work requires a potent combination of political awareness, cultural imagination and what we might call 'trickster' energy. The term is taken from Lewis Hyde, who like Omer sees the outsider, the scapegoat, the maverick brought into the centre at times of cultural change. His book *Trickster Makes This World: How disruptive imagination creates culture* highlights the role of the trickster in many native mythologies. Trickster energy is the creative force that keeps a culture in motion, mixing things up if they become stuck, restoring order if they become too chaotic, keeping the system on its toes.

Cultural leaders develop a sensitivity to the dynamics of human group interaction that at its best releases a collective group competence. In order to 'ride two paradigms' successfully, to initiate effective rather than destructive 'creative transgression', the capacity to read the existing dominant culture is essential. Persons of tomorrow have an uncanny sense of their alignment with the group – including when and how far to push their trickster energy in order to release a group's greater potential.

CHAPTER 7:

KNOWING LIKE A PERSON OF TOMORROW

The Enlightenment and Beyond

The next pillar of learning is learning to know. This is a reflective competence par excellence. In a world in which we are bombarded with information and sensation, how are we to make coherent sense? On what basis do we trust one piece of knowledge over another? How are we to operate with any degree of confidence in our knowledge when plausibility is as powerful as truth?

These are not new questions. In fact we are living inside a dominant culture of knowledge based on the answers that appeared last time they were addressed in earnest. The Enlightenment laid down the foundations of modern thought about how to make sense of the world – during a period of some 30 years from 1750 onwards, in Scotland, France and elsewhere in Europe when scholars from diverse disciplines came together to reshape understanding of how the world works.

They were responding to their own sense of a culture in transition: a dominant pattern of thinking, not least characterized by religious 'truth' and revelation, assailed by new developments in technology, new patterns of global connection (trade) and an increasingly educated and literate population ready to question received wisdom in the light of their own experience.

This led to a rich, creative inquiry over several decades, characterized in the words of Alexander Broadie (2001)[21], one of Adam Smith's successors in the chair of Logic and Rhetoric at the University of Glasgow, by:

- independent thinking and a willingness to question received truth
- tolerance for others' views and a willingness to engage with them
- a rootedness in practice and practical experience (Adam Smith learned much about the world from talking to the merchants on the Glasgow quayside)

This rich intellectual ferment led to significant conceptual breakthroughs – the discipline of modern economics, the scientific method, the elevation of reason over revelation – which in turn transformed the practical landscape and unleashed centuries of economic growth and technological progress.

However, those gains have come also at a cost. The political institutions bequeathed to us by the 18th century are suffering a twin crisis of legitimacy and competence. The legacy of the invisible hand is a combination of threats to our ecosystem that endanger our survival. And the triumph of reason and of modern science has left us alienated from the life of the spirit, searching for meaning. As Einstein is supposed to have said, we cannot solve our problems with the same level of thinking that created them.

Hence those same questions are again in play today and persons of tomorrow are following Broadie's three enabling conditions to expand the knowledge at their disposal in pursuit of effective practice. We are moving beyond an Enlightenment worldview.

Containing Multitudes

To live and prosper in a world where what counts as knowledge is in flux requires us to hold our own truth lightly. We must be able to perceive and appreciate multiple worldviews without becoming beholden to any one of them. This is a capacity to 'stand above the fray', to read the territory as if from higher ground, an extension of Harold Bridger's 'double task' that encompasses the actions of others as well as oneself.

Persons of tomorrow have this quality. They are adept at living with paradox and ambiguity. They recognize that there are numerous workable stories about the world, workable cosmologies, and acknowledge that even when we talk of universals there will always be elements of the world that remain wrapped in mystery.

These are not new thoughts. We have traditionally valued a capacity to live with paradox and incompletion as a sign of wisdom. Scott Fitzgerald wrote that "the test of a first-rate intelligence is the ability to hold two opposed ideas in the mind at the same time and still retain the ability to function". Niels Bohr found the same insight in the world of quantum physics, declaring that "the opposite of a great truth is another great truth".

The capacity to see multiple truths, to hold opposed ideas in a single mind, is in some ways a purely mental discipline. It involves reaching for a higher level of abstraction, taking a perspective that goes beyond and embraces others. But it is also, like all the capacities we name, embodied. It is lived in practice.

In a changing environment it frequently shows up as the capacity to 'ride two paradigms' (at least two!) at the same time. Persons of tomorrow are adept at displaying competence simultaneously in both the dominant culture and the emerging culture, in order to support the development of the latter. They can perform like a master in either environment, effectively playing at a 'meta-level' in which they are able to interpret the potential impact of a single move in both the dominant and the emerging culture even as they make it. Like the jazz pianist playing 5s against 13s. It is a capacity so skilful it appears invisible.

This capacity also shows up as a cultural competence, a flair for working across cultures. This is becoming increasingly important in a global, interconnected and highly mobile world. Some have dubbed it 'allophilia' – the love of the other, a position that goes well beyond 'tolerance' to a positive relishing of multiple cultures and perspectives.

The novelist Zadie Smith (2009) comments on President Obama's capacity to 'speak in tongues' – a phenomenon she observed on the campaign trail in 2008 as he subtly, and unconsciously, shifted his tone of voice and his delivery to suit the inflections of the crowd he was with. In a previous era this would likely have been seen as a mark of slipperiness and inauthenticity. But Obama, like Smith herself, is a hybrid person, a product of several cultures. It gives him a fluency that is nonetheless authentic, and entirely at home in what Bauman calls 'liquid modernity'.

The person of tomorrow echoes Walt Whitman's 'Song of Myself': "Do I contradict myself? Very well, then I contradict myself (I am large, I contain multitudes)" (Greenspan, 2005). We know many people who might fit that description and simply come across as chaotic, confused and disturbingly inconsistent. It is the combination of this quality with the other capacities named in this chapter that give it strength. The 'multitudes' are indeed 'contained' – within the capacious nature of the person of tomorrow.

Expanding Our Ways of Knowing

Part of the capacious nature of the person of tomorrow is their expansive view of what counts as valid knowledge. Modern science is founded on the conviction that in order to know the world we must remain removed from our subjective human experience and rely instead on objective, reproducible, impersonal data. This is a model of mastery and expertise: the expert as subject, the world as object.

Yet despite its solid, taken-for-granted status in the modern world, this view has been challenged in recent decades on many counts. Both modern physics and neuropsychology now accept the impossibility of neutral observation: the observer impacts the thing observed. The theory of Gaia, the earth as a living system, recontextualizes humanity as one part of a wider ecology rather than its master and cartographer: we are a part of nature, not outside it.

At the same time, we are embodied, perceiving the world through our senses. Even when we use sophisticated instruments to generate 'big data' it must still be interpreted by a human person operating as a whole being: heart, skeleton, breath, limbs all contributing their inputs to the final understanding. Neuropsychology now links us directly back to earlier explorations in somatics and hallucinogenics to greatly expand our view of how we participate in what we know. As celebrated British botanist Irene Manton told her students straining to make out subcellular features through an electron microscope, "You won't see it if you don't love it". Constructivist theories question whether knowledge about existence can ever be separated from human experience.

Adding to this paradigmatic shake-up has been a penetration into Western thought of ways of perceiving and understanding reality which set out from a fundamental assumption that all is connected and any sense of separateness of past from present, of this from that, of I from thou or us from them, is simply an illusion born of a primitive consciousness that has yet to perceive the oneness of all existence.[22]

The person of tomorrow takes an expansive view of these perspectives, recognizing that expanding our range of epistemologies and methods of inquiry can only be useful in addressing the overwhelming complexity we face. So, for example, the science of quantities has proven very powerful in apprehending those phenomena that can be reduced to distinct objects, isolated systems and inert mechanisms, where one thing can be taken to be essentially the same as another. The person of tomorrow also appreciates the science of qualities – which seeks to understand the one-off, the unique, the subjective experience and the dynamic interplay between being and its context.

To knowledge that is located, the person of tomorrow will add appreciation of collective intelligence which in some circumstances can contain knowledge in the form of emergent patterns and group consciousness. Such processes may account for those moments when seemingly out of nowhere comes the formation of a 'second sight' intuition that later proves to have been prescient. To reason and equation we add image, story and metaphor as powerful ways of encapsulating dimly perceived truth. And – thinking in terms of a participatory, subject/subject, relational world – we come to recognize that all knowledge is local, coloured and framed by culture and context. Persons of tomorrow are always wary of abstraction.

Knowing and Feeling

A particular dichotomy that has persisted since the Enlightenment is the distinction between knowing and feeling. In an Enlightenment worldview, emotions have long been the poor and benighted relations of abstraction, rationality and logic in the hierarchy of development. As behaviourist Dan Ariely believes, emotions make us irrational, confused and fall short of perfection. Perhaps that is a consequence of the fact that, in 20th-century schools, children are not given much help in becoming masters of their emotional lives. Emotions are commonly expected to be hidden, stifled, denied or shamed. Children are subtly steered into rationalization of feelings rather than being taught how to experience them and express them in effective ways.

Yet we now know from contemporary research in cognitive neuroscience, psychology and philosophy that emotions provide the frame through which we interpret and understand the world. They are as much tools for sense-making and communication as they are for 'emoting'. In Martha Nussbaum's (2001) words, "emotions shape the landscape of our mental and social lives". They "form part of our system of ethical reasoning, and we must be prepared to grapple with the messy material of grief and love, and anger and fear, and in doing so to learn what role these tumultuous experiences play in thought about the good and the just."

Persons of tomorrow are able to reconnect emotion and reason, or more correctly remember the connection that has always existed. We now know that emotions provide an important and often sensitive and reliable compass with which to judge whether we should move towards or away from some course of action and also how to assess the appropriateness of our choices and aspirations. They are an important source of feedback about the external world.

Persons of tomorrow have a full spectrum of ways of knowing where they stand and what is important that does not flow from analysis or abstraction. They are keenly aware how their emotions influence their reasoning: how, for example, fear of failure interferes with intellectual performance; or feelings of vulnerability sometimes drive choices in the direction of increased security; or hope opens up creative thinking.

They know when they are disappointed, when they are envious, lustful, loving, sad, curious, admiring, sympathetic, angry, threatened, hostile, vengeful and they have a range of options about how to respond to these states. They know how to contain emotions without damaging themselves. They know how to express them in a manner that is appropriate to any situation. A frustrated growl over a mistake feels good with an intimate but may not make sense with a boss; grief may bring teeth gnashing or hair tearing when home alone, an eloquent eulogy in public, or a tearful embrace with a friend.

As a species we come well equipped to live full emotional lives, but socialization for success in industrial civilization has largely discouraged people from learning the emotional ropes with enough sophistication to become adepts in the feelings game. Instead, many of us, especially with others, express feelings in clumsy or primitive ways. We struggle to 'keep it together', neither to over-react and make mountains out of molehills, nor under-react by understating the emotional temperature of ourselves or others and, in doing so, underestimating the potency of events.

When BP's now former CEO Tony Hayward said to the American press during the Gulf of Mexico oil spill that he thought "the environmental impact of this disaster is likely to have been very, very modest" and that he would like his "life back" it caused hurt and outrage in the people of Louisiana. His emotional illiteracy cost him his job and made BP's work orders of magnitude more difficult.

In some societies, emotional maturity is directly addressed in the education of young people and in the training of leaders. In collectivist cultures people grow up in worlds of relatively fixed relationships where instead of focusing on developing one's 'real self', separated from other real selves, people strive to develop and hone deep relational bonds. Harmony within the five cardinal relationships in Confucian etiquette – father-son, husband-wife, elder-younger, ruler-subject and friend-friend – requires the development of elaborate and flexible repertoires of feelings and responses. Japanese schools spend a considerable amount of time teaching children how to adapt flexibly to the diverse social contexts of their lives.

In a fast-paced, instantly connected world, where there will be even less time for reflection than we have at present and where an emotional misstep may have global ripples, the capacity to be in the world as a feeling being and not only as a thinking one is becoming essential.

Knowledge in Motion

One of the great challenges to classical Enlightenment thought during the 20th century came from the new mental landscape of quantum physics, the science of very small particles – quanta – of energy. Heisenberg's uncertainty principle of 1927 states that while a quantum particle in motion has both speed and location at any specific moment, we can measure only one or the other and can never be certain of both.

Similarly, for most complex processes it turns out that the more accurately we try to determine the precise state of every component, the less we can say about where the whole system might move next. Complex systems, like life itself, are fundamentally dynamic. The person of tomorrow understands this and always appreciates that knowledge is in motion.

The essential shift here is from seeing fixed stocks to seeing movement and flows. We are used to thinking in terms of stocks accumulating. So for example the metaphor of 'capital' has spread from financial circles – where it really does apply to an accumulation of resources – to social capital, natural capital, intellectual capital, reputational capital, etc., as if these were similarly measurable quantities of things. Yet it is also possible, and often more helpful, to see all these phenomena as transient forms, always in flux, flowing through complex systems.

The only distinction in nature between 'structure' and 'flow' is time: the whirlpool coexists with the stream and cannot exist without it; trees, glaciers, even mountains are in constant motion – if we had eyes to see. We can appreciate structure or flow depending on what we choose to observe. But like the figure of the two faces in profile that also looks like a vase, even though we know that both images are present we cannot see both at the same time. Western thought has tended to privilege the world of things and the properties they have rather than the invisible processes of change by which all things are just moments of relative stability. We habitually foreground structure rather than process. In so doing we limit what it is possible for us to know and apprehend about any situation.

Eastern cultures are more adept at perceiving flow and relationship, not least in respect to time itself. In the West we tend to see time as both linear and quantitative: we are always in danger of 'running out of time'. But this view of time is only one of several time-senses that human communities have developed. The Ancient Greeks distinguished between Chronos, which is quantitative and can run out, and Kairos, which is qualitative and refers to a divine sense of the pregnant or opportune moment, the 'right' time.

The Old Hebrew sense of time was also qualitative and consequential, as a medium linking time with events: "there is a time for everything under heaven".[23] Confucian time is different again. For Confucius time passes by like a river as we stand in the perpetual present. Many ancient cultures held a cyclical view of time – time as the great wheel. Psychological time also has a quality – we have all experienced the state of utter absorption in which hours seem to pass in minutes (and, alas, the opposite!). Many of the more esoteric ways to expand what we consider as knowledge – ritual, meditation, trance, movement, etc. – are explicitly designed to impact the quality of time.

When time is seen as an endless, infinite flow we are more likely to think in terms of cycles of birth, death ('creative destruction') and renewal rather than linear progress towards 'success'. Given that human systems are always conscious of their mortality, this view of time as cyclical is a large part of some cultures' capacity to cultivate fearlessness towards death. In other words, this shift in thinking helps to enable the courage we have spoken about in previous chapters.

Maps and Compasses

In seeking to make sense of a dynamic, changing landscape it is useful to find at least the best map of the territory you can, and preferably also a compass. The person of tomorrow is likely to be familiar with a wide range of specific tools and thinking techniques which have the common characteristic of encouraging a more expansive view of any situation. These include thinking in terms of systems, for example, or of different time horizons, using alternative scenarios and narratives, adopting multiple perspectives (like de Bono's (1986) six thinking hats and Gardner's (1983) multiple intelligences), using dilemma thinking to avoid false choices, or more open conversational processes to access multiple stakeholder viewpoints (encounter, open space, dialogue, appreciative inquiry, world café).

The list of techniques is (almost!) endless but to focus on them would be to miss the point. In persons of tomorrow their use arises and flows from a desire always to expand their awareness, to explore more of the context, to adopt a broader perspective, a longer-term perspective, a perspective that recognizes the humanity in any system. Long dominated by reductionism, new capacities are emerging for pattern recognition, both/and thinking, and figure/ground recognition that can perceive the part without losing the whole.

Persons of tomorrow are not afraid of complexity – indeed they thrive on it. They know that the secret to not becoming overwhelmed is paradoxically to live in the unfolding situation as fully as they can. Like the children's bear hunt, they know that they can't go round it, can't go over it, can't ignore it: they are ready to go through it.

At the same time, a sense of direction can help, or at least the presence of some personal lodestar to maintain your bearings in a complex world. Steve Rayner (2007), Director of the Institute for Science, Innovation and Society at Oxford University, picks up on one aspect of this challenge: how any layperson can discriminate wheat from chaff in the swirl of technical science published today. He suggests that what is needed for those without detailed technical expertise is 'scientific connoisseurship'. By this he means a capacity to make informed judgements about scientific claims and to be able to judge the competence and credibility of individuals and institutions presented as scientific experts or authorities.

It is a nice term, and a useful one. Connoisseurship implies judgement, taste, subtle appreciation. A capacity to make judgements about the unknown, based on incomplete, conflicting or incomprehensible knowledge. This is a human capacity, a capacity of whole persons, likely to draw on all their ways of knowing. There is no coding algorithm for connoisseurship in any field.

Mark Cosgrove, Artistic Director of the Encounters Bristol International Film Festival, talks explicitly about the 'compass' he uses to frame his connoisseur's knowledge.[24] This too is a nice and a useful image. During two weeks in August each year he has to assess hundreds of entries for selection in the festival. He rates them not on any linear scale from 1 to 10, or even against a matrix of different qualities. Instead he locates them in relation to the space implied by four compass points, each represented by a different work of art or moment in art that has a particular resonance for him or encapsulates a particular quality. None of the compass points derives from film. The famous moment at a 1966 concert in Manchester where an audience member shouted 'Judas!' at Bob Dylan's electric set is Cosgrove's 'true north'. It stands for a quality – the artist trusting his own integrity and growth and challenging his audience to grow with him – that Cosgrove appreciates in other works.

The person of tomorrow is adept at finding tools, frameworks, models that help to expand the depth and breadth of perspective available in any situation in order to make better sense of it. No representation is taken to be definitive. There will always be more to discover, always room for another rationality, for second and third thoughts. What is more important, as the map continues to evolve, is to be in possession of a reliable compass. Persons of tomorrow know their own true north.

CHAPTER 8:

ORGANIZING PERSONS OF TOMORROW

The Setting: Places to Grow

We now turn to the fourth pillar of learning: learning to do. The next chapter will examine the kind of action learning that we believe will help to develop the 21st-century competencies and the one after that will suggest how best to get started.

But first we consider organizational form. As we have seen, particularly through the shadowing encounters with leaders and chief executives referred to in Chapter 4, the nature of the organizational setting has a big impact on how the people who populate it develop. And vice versa. People and setting develop together.

We know that, largely driven by technology and the faster, ubiquitous flow of knowledge and information, dominant industrial models of organization based around hierarchy are starting to adapt – giving way to more networked forms with distributed centres of authority. The plethora of recent policy and business books on 'management 2.0', 'disorganization as the new organization' and the like are full of suggestions offered with breathless urgency for how to introduce disruption and creative innovation into structures that have become too big, too complacent, too rigid, too set in their ways.

Mostly the motivation is the search for greater effectiveness in a changing world. Less remarked upon is the need to free up these structures specifically to allow for the ways of being, knowing and being together favoured by persons of tomorrow. Frederic Laloux's *Reinventing Organizations* is rare in explicitly addressing the need for people and organization to develop together. It also catalogues numerous useful practices – small acts of creative transgression? – that can be introduced in any organization.

There is an equally lively debate about legal forms. Persons of tomorrow, following their own true north, are becoming frustrated with the limitations of the simple for-profit/not-for-profit split. They are actively exploring new legal forms for social enterprises seeking to blend these models to retain the energy of the market without the distortions of shareholder demands: Community Interest Companies in the UK, for example, or the B-Corporation and the Low-Profit Limited Liability Company (L3C) in the United States.

It is not surprising to find persons of tomorrow, those exploring their own creative edge and catalysing such a spirit in the people around them, looking to work together in looser, more purposeful organizational forms. As natural boundary spanners they find themselves gravitating towards loosely coupled, temporary, collaborative, cross-disciplinary structures. Many of these models take inspiration from the world of the arts: ever since the 1960s other sectors have looked enviously at their fluency in the use of 'temporary systems' like theatre and film production.

Establishing an organizational context for working together is one aspect of the challenge – and relates to the previous chapter on culture, group dynamics and 'being together'. A parallel challenge is to marry that way of working with a suitable legal form and business model in order to interact effectively with the money economy. This chapter offers some thoughts and sources of hope and encouragement on both aspects. However, it must be recognized that the latter part of the challenge in particular is very much work in progress in today's dominant culture.

The Promise of Adhocracy

It was the management theorist Henry Mintzberg (1979) who coined the term 'adhocracy' for the loosely coupled, temporary, collaborative structures that seem to favour (and be favoured by) persons of tomorrow. He identified it as the only structure suited to the prevailing operating environments of the late 20th century and the trend towards extreme complexity, confusion and ever-changing demands. "Adhocracy", he wrote, "is the only structure for environments becoming more complex and demanding of innovation, and for technical systems becoming more sophisticated and highly automated." Adhocracies are designed for the extraordinary: "adhocracy is not competent at doing ordinary things".

Aside from its flexibility and adaptability to creative demands, the form also nurtures other qualities essential for persons of tomorrow. In contrast with all forms of bureaucracy, adhocracy restores the importance of person over role. It is a form in which the unique identity of each person in the organization matters: put a different person in the same role and the nature of the whole organization will change.

At the same time this puts increased pressure on the individual. Richard Eckersley (2004) refers to "agentic overload" where the demand to "be all you can be" all day, everyday and in whatever setting becomes a source of stress and burnout. Thomas Friedman (2011) warns job hunters in today's tight market that they will need to "add value every hour, every day — more than a worker in India, a robot or a computer". Employers will ask of applicants: "can he or she help my company adapt by not only doing the job today but also reinventing the job for tomorrow? And can he or she adapt with all the change, so my company can adapt and export more into the fastest-growing global markets? In today's hyperconnected world, more and more companies cannot and will not hire people who don't fulfil those criteria." A heavy demand with significant psychological costs.

The sociologist Richard Sennett (2006) echoes the point. He observes that the "cultural ideal" demanded by many of the institutions of the new capitalism, built as they are around highly creative, footloose, hard-working, restless individuals, "damages many of the people who inhabit them".

Mintzberg too characterized the adhocracy form as typically populated by young, highly qualified, ambitious and self-confident personnel ready to accept enormous variations in work time and work load. Inevitably this environment takes its toll. Though often idealized as the form that supports entrepreneurial creativity, of all organizational forms adhocracy is also the most Darwinian: "supportive of the strong so long as they remain strong, and destructive of the weak". Perhaps that is why the term, and the form, has never really caught on.

And Its Dangers

This kind of loose, networked form is highly conducive to evoking and therefore honing the competencies for liquid modernity and powerful times. But the strain it puts on people is a potentially fatal flaw. We have seen something of this in our own researches. Some of the most impressive performers were to be found operating in fragile organizational forms – and the strain of maintaining the balance between structure and security on the one hand and freedom and creativity on the other was evident.

The principal reason for people to come together in an organization is usually to get something done. The purpose of any organizational form is to provide a means of collective agency. Yet what we fail to notice is that these settings also serve a psychological purpose. In the words of Don Michael (1973a), "one of the functions organizations perform is to buffer the individual member from the impact of the chaotic interrelation of everything to everything. Ideally organizations free the member to deal with just so much of the environment as their intellect and psyche permit."

In other words, the organization provides a zone of competence and predictability, a safe space to protect the psyche in a world threatening to overwhelm it. We would argue today that as the conditions of fluid modernity pervade more and more of the space in which people have to operate, this protection is both illusory (we can no longer keep the complexity at bay) and undesirable if it prevents the kind of engagement with the real world that we need in order to grow. Further, there is some concern that the loose, ad hoc forms that are now coming to prominence inhibit the development of longer-term relationships and moral commitment (one of the criticisms of the start-up culture of Silicon Valley).

One response is to improve the capacities of individuals to work in such environments. Gerard Fairtlough (2007), for example, suggests that critical to effectiveness in these new organizational forms are "interpersonal process skills, the special skills for empathic dialogue, teamwork and mutual respect". A focus group we conducted with young social entrepreneurs in San Francisco in 2011 emphasized the need for more attention in management schools on the self-care and interpersonal skills needed to thrive in the fast-paced, multi-tasking, networked world in which they find themselves (O'Hara, 2011). These needs are reflected in the meteoric rise of personal and professional coaching, but we notice that much of this work focuses on individuals and so is unlikely to deliver mastery of group and organizational dynamics.

We welcome the growing awareness that the demands of the new economy and a global context changing at bewildering speed are placing new kinds of pressure on people for which they are ill-prepared. But a response that simply provides us with the resources better to survive damaging organizational forms and cultures is only treating the symptoms.

Our own practical work has generally focused on creating a supportive counter-culture within existing organizations and then enabling that to grow. In these cases we are usually responding to a cry for help from those in existential pain in their current settings.

But we also aspire to discover the stable and sustainable organizational form of the future that will best enable the development of the essential human qualities that characterize persons of tomorrow.

The remainder of this chapter addresses three aspects of that development: creative ways of working together, the organizational form that might support those ways, and the relationship with the market economy that will allow money to flow through that form without distorting its essence or purpose.

The Producer

As temporary, networked, ad hoc, project-based structures have become more common, so we have come to appreciate the critical role often played in such ventures by a 'producer' figure.

It is a role that has come to prominence in the world of arts and culture, where practising artists value the presence of an intermediary between their work and the world. At its simplest the producer might handle the mundane aspects of commerce or legal niceties, providing space for the artist to concentrate on what they do best. But the role usually stretches into becoming a creative partner, a sounding board, a coach, mentor, editor – providing both the necessary container for creative activity and equally necessary outreach to a world of relationships beyond. Essentially they take responsibility for marshalling resources (broadly defined) around a creative idea.

For larger collaborations between partners, the producer role becomes central – effectively providing in one person and a distinctive set of competencies the essential elements of structure we normally associate with 'organization'.

This notion of 'production' is therefore very much more than what we find in the professional leadership literature, where there is usually a distinction made between those who lead and those who produce. The familiar entrepreneurial chain consists of a visionary leader who has an image of what might be, a designer who figures out how to bring the vision into concrete existence and a producer who realizes the design. The process seems to work for the production of certain kinds of things – products, processes, changes that can be visualized ahead of time, with little concern for the changing circumstances into which they will be launched. But if what we imagine must enter a future we cannot predict then this design and production chain may end up missing its mark.

The familiar chain of vision-design-production needs to be reconceptualized if organizations are to keep pace with a shifting world. The producer in the arts world occupies all three roles at different times, navigating between the bold vision of a new idea and its realization in the world. As Kate Tyndall (2002) says in her book *The Producers*, he or she "might be the chief executive of a well-developed organization with specialist teams focusing on particular aspects of the producing task, or they might function solo or lead a small or medium-sized team. As producer, however, they hold the full picture, and are responsible for the successful intersection of all the forces at work in order to realize the idea in the most brilliant way possible."

Helen Marriage, for example, describes well the protective role she took on over five years in bringing the 12m-high Sultan's Elephant to the streets of London in the spring of 2006. She was responsible for bringing together the troupe of puppeteers, negotiating with the city authorities, securing the funding and a whole host of other things. Clearly this one figure effectively played the role we traditionally expect to be filled by 'organization': "The deal we did was that if they [the funders] bought into the idea of the project we would guarantee to make it happen. It is the producer's role to take responsibility" (Leicester, 2014).

The opening ceremony for the London 2012 Olympics was a classic creative 'production', brought together over several years, encompassing a huge variety of inputs and a cast including 7,500 volunteers. At its core was a small creative team led by film director Danny Boyle, all of whom had worked together in different combinations before on other projects. Boyle also took on the role of liaising with the politicians and others with an interest, mediating between the work and the world.

At the heart of the project was a temporary space in which everyone was encouraged to bring their full potential to play. In the words of one member, writer Frank Cottrell Boyce, "Danny created a room where no one was afraid to speak, no one had to stick to their own specialism, no one was afraid of sounding stupid or talking out of turn. He restored us to the people we were before we made career choices – to when we were just wondering."

Not surprisingly, successful producers need to display the 21st-century competencies in abundance. Tyndall's book provides a series of interviews (a form of shadowing) with a variety of such figures. They describe qualities like a sense of balance: "It's the producer's role to be the bridge between the work and the world, the artist and the audience" (Michael Morris). A capacity to be supremely attentive: "What I am doing is based in the powerful, intense, productive moment" (Paul Heritage). And at the same time a recognition of just how much this role demands of you: "I'm fuelled up on adrenalin and probably heading for an early grave... But unexpected and unwelcome things can be interesting. It's like that bit in a show that creeps up on you and smacks you. It either throws you off balance, or it can be the very thing that propels the experience to a new dimension" (David Jubb).

It is surprising how important a skilled producer is to making an adhocracy effective. It is a role that is often overlooked in putting together a project team. Some mistakenly see it as no more than project management. That approach worked in the 20th century and works today in conditions of stability, certainty and the coordination of skillsets based on 'technical rationality' (to use Donald Schön's phrase). But today's looser forms call on more diverse qualities – such as those described in this book.

Robust Adhocracy

Somewhere between the dangerous, short-term, burnout-prone model of the networked adhocracy and the space-holding of the 21st-century producer, persons of tomorrow still crave the robust organizational setting that will develop rather than constrain them.

The search is on, therefore, for an organizational form that can nurture individual identity, imagination and initiative at the same time as it provides buffering against intolerable levels of uncertainty and the functional limitation of formlessness so that effective collective action is possible.

Just like the person of tomorrow, it is possible to sense this kind of organization emerging in practice – we know it when we see it. The theory that underpins the practice, however, still seems to be in its early days. One of the most hopeful studies is the investigation by Max Boisot (2011) of the ATLAS experiment with the Large Hadron Collider at CERN. It is a rare example of an adhocracy working at scale and Boisot's analysis provides clues for how to make any adhocracy more robust.

The ATLAS experiment, one of those conducted at CERN to verify the existence of the Higgs boson, is a remarkable collaboration of over 3,000 scientists working for 174 research institutions spread across 38 countries. Boisot has researched the operating structure, leadership and management regimes in great depth. He concludes that the form is a loose adhocracy. It is held together by nothing more than a Memorandum of Understanding – a gentleman's agreement with no legal force that "facilitates a flexible bottom-up process of self-organization". The structures leave maximum space for creative collaboration and exploration in the search for new knowledge at the boundaries of our theoretical understanding of the universe.

Boisot's study of ATLAS, *Collisions and Collaboration*, explores the experiment, chapter by chapter, from many different perspectives – management, leadership, procurement, planning, design, culture, ICT, commercialization and big science, etc. The conclusions of the study overall are important, far-reaching and profound.

Most interesting from the perspective of organizational form are his findings about what has enabled the ATLAS adhocracy to scale to such size, to remain stable over such a long period, to design and work with one of the largest, most ambitious and most complex experimental machines ever built, to absorb the huge sums of money associated with 'big science' and yet retain its capacity to operate as a real human system engaged in creative exploration: much closer to Danny Boyle's artistic team than to a traditional research bureaucracy.

Several critical features help to bind the numbers of people together. One is the shared scientific goal: finding the Higgs boson. A second is the shared culture of science in general (the integrity of measurement, etc.) and of high energy physics in particular. CERN itself, as part of the mix, provides a "keystone actor endowed with some kind of legal status" – a necessary "nightwatchman bureaucracy" that sits on the margins of the collaboration to handle the ordinary aspects while the adhocracy can concentrate on the extraordinary.

Perhaps the most significant factor is what Boisot calls a "boundary object" – something stable around which all the other actors and factors can coordinate their actions. This is the particle detector itself, the piece of kit that lies at the heart of the experiment and on the results of which the whole collaboration is based. None of those involved can argue with the detector or the laws of physics that it is designed to reveal.

What allows this large-scale, shared, collective human endeavour to manifest around the detector is trust and loyalty. "Loyalty", writes Boisot, "is the indispensable binding agent... Loyalty to shared purposes, norms, and values allows a loosely coupled adhocracy such as ATLAS to gravitate around an infrastructure of boundary objects that helps to coordinate the actions of its members with little in the way of formal managerial authority."

Sociologist Martin Albrow has gone further in exploring the central role that trusting human relationship plays in holding together any collective 'human being' in the confusing operating environment of the 21st century. In view of the critical role of trust, Albrow calls this an 'integrity'.

The concept of an integrity explicitly challenges previous notions of organization that assume people can be brought together and integrated into a single powerful entity – with a single creed, 'singing from the same hymn sheet' – capable of imposing its will on the world.

Albrow instead accepts a fluid modernity, in which we all participate in and belong to many different groupings at the same time (we will not give our soul to the company alone). Those groupings are less imposing their will on the world than simply keeping themselves upright amidst the turbulence. They maintain a sense of identity and moral purpose not by virtue of mission statements or tightly controlled 'branding' but as a consequence of a myriad exchanges of meaning with their environment over time.

An integrity can be formed by any group of people that has come together to maintain a sense of values-based purpose over time. It is this sense of purpose and values that holds the entity together rather than any formal constitution or set of black letter rules (more like a family, a social movement or a group of friends than a corporation or even a members' club).

Individual players manage their personal contributions and demands and the emergent results of that ripple through ever-wider cycles of involvement. The entity self-organizes, coordinated by the shared sense of purpose individually interpreted. And the entity in turn is constantly negotiating its relationship with other entities and with a changing external world. These negotiations occur around four critical dimensions:

- *sovereignty*: the control of resources
- *recognition*: identity, how the entity is regarded, reputation
- *reciprocity*: the web of relationships and mutual obligations
- *agency*: the capacity to get things done, to realize something in the world

We have found this idea of integrity to be extremely valuable in effectively establishing boundary conditions for a space in which persons of tomorrow can express their 21st-century competencies. As a template for organizing (rather than a static 'organization') it allows any group, at any scale, effectively to create in the relationships between them the necessary structure otherwise embodied in a specific producer role. We have found it a particularly effective framework for enabling individuals working within an organization to support each other in growing a counter-culture able to support a new vision of practice.

The clear basis in shared values and moral purpose feeds psychological stamina and persistence. The prominence of agency as one of the four critical dimensions through which the entity interacts with the world puts a premium on participation and engagement. And the fact that the whole is conceived in terms of organizing – again verb not noun – always adapting to and negotiating its place in a changing environment, acknowledges the value of maintaining an effective tactical relationship with the dominant culture.

Money at the Margins

A critical element in that dominant culture is the market economy and the role of money in all our lives. It is striking how people looking for organizational settings in tune with their values and aspirations describe those options less in terms of culture and organizational form and more in terms of legal structure: private enterprise, public bureaucracy, classic not-for-profit charitable activity, and an increasingly varied field of social enterprise and other hybrid forms.

What these legal structures determine are not ways of working but the relationship between the collective endeavour at the organization's heart and the economy of money: ownership, profit, distribution, taxation and so on.

These issues have come to occupy centre stage, we believe, partly because we have elevated the economy of money above all other patterns of valuation. Bill Sharpe (2010) argues in *Economies of Life: Patterns of health and wealth* that any pattern of shared valuing coordinated by a currency is an economy. In other words, there are as many economies as there are patterns of value.

The person of tomorrow, therefore, adept at balancing multiple perspectives, will pay particular attention to the relationship between economies. In this regard money is particularly powerful. It is the currency in an economy of trade and exchange. It allows us to remove things from one system and context, one pattern of valuing, and place them in another. But whilst we might in this way create value in one economy, we might at the same time, if we are not careful and attentive, be undermining other value systems.

Science is itself an economy in which the currency coordinating it is measurement. Vast sums of money flow through science, but none of it is allowed to 'buy' a particular set of falsified results. Sport is another economy in which the rules about what constitutes a score enable us to coordinate activity between different games. Again lots of money can flow through the system – but you cannot bribe the referee to award a goal when the ball never crossed the line. We expect a doctor to place primary value on our health and will feel worried if we find they are incentivized to provide treatments regardless of our condition.

Sharpe suggests that, unless the principal value at the heart of a collaborative endeavour is to make money, the best rule is to keep money at the margins. We always have a choice about where to net out the value of our activities in the money economy, about which transactions to charge for. We should allow money to flow through the system, but keep it distanced from the critical relationships and transactions that define the value-creating system we are most interested in.

From this follows the need to become clearer about the patterns of valuing that concern us in any collective endeavour. Persons of tomorrow will be comfortable with the idea that there are many economies in play, and that any activity they undertake together will involve a 'constellation' of different value patterns which in some sense will be configured by the intentions of the group. They will have their own compass points, their own sense of the rewards they expect from the work.

The difference is that this conversation will not only be about business models, finance and legal form. Typically, money is seen as the principal energy flowing through any sustainable system of activity. It is either an end in itself (traditional business) or the means of achieving other impacts through its redistribution or purposing for good (charity, mission-driven enterprise, etc.). That frame is blind to the psychological strain most forms of organization now expose us to. A robust organization must also consider what we call 'results on the inside' – the qualities of life that are developed and enjoyed in common simply through participation in any shared endeavour.

This is a missing piece in the organizational jigsaw. Organization is a means of getting things done. But it is also a way of living together. The value of being in an organizational setting that embodies the qualities of persons of tomorrow can only be gained through participation and experience. It cannot be bought. It is like learning a language: the only way to do so is to practise, in the company of others. You cannot be part of an organization that privileges results on the inside without yourself being transformed.

CHAPTER 9:

PERSONS OF TOMORROW IN ACTION

Becoming Through Doing

Throughout this book we have insisted that the 21st-century competencies will be developed and expressed through action. Indeed, we have adopted that as the very definition of competence: "the ability to meet important challenges in life in a complex world".

Previous chapters have outlined the capacities, the qualities, the attributes of those we have called 'persons of tomorrow'. These are in effect the enabling conditions for effective action, for the demonstration of competence. As the Delors Commission rightly saw, we need to learn how to be, how to be together, how to know – and how to organize ourselves for collective activity. But it is through action that the resulting competencies will be expressed and demonstrated, and through a process of action learning that they will be developed.

If we are right that our times require us to develop or at least rediscover new competencies, it would seem reasonable to assume that a developmental agenda would be a high priority wherever learning takes place. The paradox, however, is that whilst we have never faced a steeper learning curve, training budgets are down, time devoted to learning is regarded as a luxury, and few people in busy organizations think they can afford the time for the slow process of psychological growth and development.

Fortunately we believe the 21st-century competencies are latent within all human beings, and can be evoked or called forth in any of us if we find ourselves in the right setting and given the right enabling conditions. They are not extraordinary and are part of the rich human repertoire. They do not need to be 'taught' as such – so long as an individual has the capacity to perform the 'double task' necessary to learn from experience and a supportive mentor or guide to reinforce the learning.

There is no need to go to school. There is no textbook to study and recall in examination conditions. You cannot (easily) enrol in a course of study at university to develop these competencies, and you should not expect to be awarded a certificate when you do. They are genuinely 'drawn out' from us (to recall the root meaning of 'educate'). They are discovered, developed and expressed in action.

John Seeley Brown, executive turned educational reform advocate, takes a similar view (in Collins *et al.*, 1991). He suggests that the advanced skills needed for success in these times require learning through experience. This is the kind of learning undertaken for hundreds of years in the ateliers of great artists and in the labs of scientists until their eclipse by modern behavioural instructional design. Ateliers immerse would-be artists, scientists and craft workers in day-to-day work on real projects under the supervision of masters.

Seeley Brown suggests that the important part of this process is the cognitive apprenticeship it provides, by which the intricacies of the creative production process are internalized through exposure and repetition. Persons of tomorrow develop their advanced human capacities and express their 21st-century competencies through a similar engagement with the complex higher order challenges that cannot be addressed at today's level of consciousness. They are developed and demonstrated through experience.

Nor are they learned alone. These new competencies are developed through processes of social and cultural learning, ideally in the company of people who exhibit them already. Practising cultural leadership and transformative innovation will by definition transgress the dominant culture. So this kind of learning must take place in the liminal spaces at the margins, on the borders, at the edge, under the radar, out of the sight lines of conventional institutions.

In short, for those ready to develop the 21st-century competencies we see three essential conditions:

- you cannot learn without action, gaining direct experience
- you cannot learn without reflection, the capacity to perform the double task (mentors can help)
- and you cannot learn alone: no solo climbers

But what kind of action? The OECD definition offers three significant pointers. It talks of 'challenges' which suggests that we need to stretch ourselves beyond what we know how to do. It further specifies that these need to be 'important' challenges, so our action needs to be related to something meaningful and potentially impactful for ourselves and others. Finally, the definition refers to the 'complex world', which invites us to engage complexity as part of the challenge. These are all essential elements – on which we elaborate below.

Recall too that 21st-century competencies are qualities of persons as a whole. Being, being together, knowing and doing are intimately and inevitably connected. Whilst this chapter is focused on 'doing', our actions will also be an expression of who we are and what we see, a product of our reading of the landscape. They will flow from our new-found literacies – psychological, cultural, epistemic – and our capacity to bring our expanded selves, individually and collectively, to the challenges of the times.

We may need to prepare ourselves for this kind of action. So this chapter explores settings in which we can develop our awareness, tune up our competencies and rehearse our actions before we go on stage and play for real. These might be sites of learning or of experiment, places and spaces where the three conditions listed above are satisfied, if only temporarily. The next chapter will explore how to create and sustain these conditions for yourself, in your organization or other professional context, wherever it is that you feel the need to move from rehearsal to performance.

What Kind of Action?

In today's culture the call to action can easily take on a neurotic intensity: "don't just sit there, do something!" There is impatience with reflection and conversation. 'Talking shops' are denigrated, think tanks are rebranding as 'do tanks' to escape reproach.

Persons of tomorrow are more circumspect. Whilst acknowledging that they will inevitably be acting on partial and incomplete knowledge, and that the outcomes are uncertain, they nevertheless seek so far as possible to adhere to the Hippocratic Oath taken by doctors: first, do no harm.

That means they are choosy about the actions they take: 'it is better than nothing' is not a phrase you are likely to hear from their lips. This will come as no surprise to those who have read this far and can imagine embodied qualities of humility, patience, courage and faith in the future in action.

To express and develop 21st-century competencies requires us to immerse ourselves in a particular quality of situation where standard approaches will fail, or have already been tried and failed in the past. We need to be put to the test, to stretch ourselves. But in what dimensions? And how should we choose? The following pages offer some suggestions.

Messy and Complex

It is feeling out of our depth that will encourage us to express competencies we have not required in order to be successful up to this point. Ideally one should find a situation that is complex, messy, paradoxical, difficult to make sense of, intractable at the current level of action and understanding – something that will obviously demand of us more than we have readily to hand.

Such circumstances should not be hard to find. Bookshelves are groaning with literature about 'wicked problems' and 'social messes'. They arise in situations where there are many factors involved, everything impacts everything else, the stakes are high, even the 'facts' are uncertain or disputed, there are elephants in the room that are not spoken of, values are in dispute, unintended consequences are likely, previous interventions have failed and the outcome of further interventions is highly uncertain. And so on.

Peter Senge (1990) talks about such issues being complex in three ways:

- dynamically complex: cause and effect are interdependent and far apart in space and time
- socially complex: actors involved have different perspectives and interests
- generatively complex: the future state of the complex of issues is fundamentally unfamiliar and undetermined

These are the kinds of situations that are not amenable to the simple application of 20th-century technical skills and approaches. Breaking them down into manageable fragments (the reductionist mode) will not work, because each element is inextricably part of the whole. Rigorous data collection and econometrics, even if it produces a perfect 'solution', will not work because that solution is utterly impractical in the world of day-to-day politics, finance and organization.

The best way to address such problems is not to reduce them to fit our existing competencies, but to expand ourselves to encompass more of the complexity of the situation. Not to work on solving a set of abstractions derived from the situation but to immerse ourselves in the experience of the situation itself – to see what it evokes, and what can be learned when we bring our full range of intelligences to bear, individually and collectively.

Hopeful and Wise

Such circumstances are likely to feel overwhelming. We are not suggesting that everyone should immediately immerse themselves in something as all-encompassing as solving world poverty. There is a further level of discernment required – both about the scale and more importantly the quality of the action to be attempted.

Recall our chosen definition of competence: 'the ability to meet important challenges in life in a complex world'. What characterizes 'an important challenge in life' is very much up to the individuals involved and will depend on their context at the time of asking. Recall our discussion of Antonovsky's conditions for 'coherence' in Chapter 3 in which he emphasizes the emotional motivation that helps us make sense of a challenge because it has meaning for us and is worth our effort in taking on. Thus the challenge chosen will arise partly from its complexity (as described above), but will also be resonant at an emotional level. It will mean something to us. It is likely to be something that has been frustrating us for a while, something we would dearly like to achieve but don't know how to. The action chosen will be aspirational, full of hope.

Hence we suggest the following essential characteristics for the kind of action most likely to encourage you to express the 21st-century competencies. It should be:

- inspiring
- capable of inspiring others
- desirable but out of reach (and therefore requiring transformational competence to deliver)

The action can start at any level and any scale, however large the circumstance it is intended to address. What will allow the impact of the initial action to grow is not its scale but its quality.

As described in Chapter 6, the beginning of cultural leadership is always a small act of creative transgression. It is small because transgression on a larger scale amounts to revolution and human systems resist this level of change as long as they can. The smaller – and cheaper – it is, the easier it is for others to follow the lead. It must also be transgressive to some degree because in order to shift the culture we must challenge it: we must do something counter-cultural. And it is creative, rather than merely disruptive, because it appeals in some ways to the culture's deeper values, its 'better self', and it is focused on the future.

Such work requires a potent combination of political awareness and cultural imagination. This is the combination we find in the 'producer' role: the artful introduction of the new in the presence of the old, bringing the future system into being whilst accounting for actions to funders and board members who are embedded in a culture that the actions are designed to challenge. This ability is itself a 21st-century competence, developed through experience.

It is the quality found in small acts of creative transgression. It took a new headteacher at the Hornsey School for Girls in North London, for example, to turn off the school bell for a fortnight as an experiment. There were complaints at first and resistance, but over time it dramatically improved the environment, brought out all kinds of unanticipated beneficial community behaviours and the bell has never been restored (Broadbent, 2006).

In cases like these the intervention is subtle, small-scale, low-cost. But to the instigators it is an initial intervention in tune with a much larger vision. Rosa Parks's refusal to move was a quiet stand for equality. Turning off the school bell was a shift towards shared responsibility rather than control. In the economy of meaning these small acts are highly significant interventions – and are recognized as such. They evoke a resource in us that lies hidden in a culture under strain. They inspire and intrigue. They attract. And because they do, they scale and spread naturally acting like 'social acupuncture'.

Above all they are what we call 'wise initiatives'. Wise because they are consciously designed as initial probes in a complex system. We know that you cannot control a complex system, only disturb it. They are small-scale disturbances, not too disruptive, designed to prompt learning about the next move. They are wise in the sense that we are unlikely to regret them – either because of the waste of resource or the disruption caused by unintended consequences. And they will be wise in proportion to the depth and breadth of context we have taken into account before taking the initiative.

Patient and Reflective

Taking action will kick start a learning cycle. Indeed, that is all it is designed to do initially. The action is a trigger to reflection and learning – not something that is simply 'delivered' and then we move on.

The radical Brazilian educator Paulo Freire (1998) drew a critical distinction between reflective action and mere 'activism'. "Critical reflection on practice is a requirement of the relationship between theory and practice. Otherwise theory becomes simply 'blah, blah, blah', and practice, pure activism." In other words, meaningful action in complex systems must be embedded in the culture of the reflective practitioner: we must remain aware of our inescapable vulnerability to self-deception and blind spots and be faithful to an intention to learn from the impact of our actions upon the situation we address and upon ourselves.

This is one of the reasons why we say there should be 'no solo climbers'. By definition blind spots are invisible to us and yet they often point us to where the new learning resides. It helps to have a co-conspirator to reflect with from time to time, so that each can coach the other. Maintaining a regular schedule of meetings through the development of a project is useful. It becomes part of the discipline: we will meet and talk whether we need to or not. It is when you are meeting for no purpose that surprising discovery and insight may be more likely to occur.

One of the things likely to come up is just how difficult it is to maintain the coherence of a novel process against a background of so much noise, confusion and – often – pain. The hopeful quality of the endeavour will also likely start to attract attention and the tactful skills we associated earlier in this book with the role of 'producer' will need to be employed and developed in order to welcome others into the process without damaging the integrity of the whole.

Working in this way, at whatever scale, provides cultural leadership. For those under stress a culture that expresses hope rather than fear is likely to be both attractive and revelatory. As that culture starts to generate not only good energy but also impressive results, the time will come when it will make sense to 'come out of stealth mode' and seek to influence the influential.

Recall also the injunction about time. In our dominant culture it is always a potential source of anxiety. Be aware of that, and do not succumb. It has always taken 40 years to get to the Promised Land, and old ideas have to wither along the way. Slowly but surely is a piece of ancient wisdom – especially worth recalling in our 24/7, always-on culture. Aesop's fable about the tortoise and the hare was not just an entertainment: it was a teaching.

The Master of Go

Finally, we see in persons of tomorrow an expanded strategic view of how to achieve satisfaction in a complex, shifting environment. They have an intuitive sense of what we might call an Eastern view of strategy.

The Western view is familiar. We set our goal, plan our route, marshal our resources and execute the journey from A to B. We impose ourselves on the world to create something we call 'change'. The Eastern view, most eloquently and timelessly expressed in Sun Tzu's *The Art of War* is very different. The highest triumph of strategy in this view is to 'win the war without fighting'.

What underpins this approach is a very different appreciation of reality as an ever-changing landscape that evolves and emerges under forces we only dimly understand. David Bohm (1980) called it the 'implicate order' that can become 'explicate'.

François Jullien (2004), in perhaps the best modern exposition of this way of thinking, talks about the 'potentialities' in the landscape.

On this view, strategy is not about imposing one's goals on the external world, but instead about reading the landscape with such exquisite distinction that you can see the potential for what is going to happen next: the future potential of the present moment.

John Kay's (2010) book *Obliquity* draws on this same centuries-old tradition – winning your way through surprising and indirect means; through a more nuanced reading of the landscape. It is about tact, timing, cunning and outwitting obstacles rather than relying on brute force to overcome them. Persons of tomorrow have this strategic appreciation in their repertoire. They are adept at playing chess – knowing the rules, thinking ahead – but they are also masters of Go, the more subtle ancient Chinese game of strategy, where the personal capacities of the players such as patience, balance, flexibility and resolve, aesthetics and understanding are paramount.

You win the battle without fighting not by seeking to impose change, but simply by placing yourself in the landscape with a deeper awareness of the present and a greater strategic vision than your opponent. They end up in a dead end, cornered, on the low ground, disadvantaged – and surrender.

There is likewise an ethical component in this way of reading the landscape. Eastern strategy values winning without fighting also because of high and equal respect for the warrior on both sides of the battle. It sits inside an egalitarian appreciation of human dignity. And its ethics come from that place rather than from a set of written rules.

Contemporary philosophers have written about the distinction between defensive and creative ethics. The former is about 'doing the right thing' according to a set of predetermined rules and procedures. The latter is about doing the right thing in a specific circumstance, in the moment, acknowledging the uniqueness of every situation. It is 'creative' in the sense that a decision must be created rather than computed. It is risky in that the individual concerned must take personal responsibility for their judgement and behaviour.

But it is of a piece with everything else that has been written in this chapter – and a responsibility that the person of tomorrow does not shy from.

Theatres for Action Learning

The 21st-century competencies are developed and expressed through the kinds of action described above. We also know that some settings are more conducive to evoking them than others. So what settings might we place ourselves in to develop our literacies and our awareness of the landscape and to play and experiment with an expanding sense of our own qualities of being, knowing and being together?

We are not likely to find the right conditions by going back to school. When we asked the people we shadowed how they had developed the competencies they now display not one pointed to their formal education. Though each was highly credentialed in some field they agreed that the way they operate in their various professional settings was not learned in school.

That comes as no surprise. It is now a widely shared view that formal education, especially higher education, is falling short of turning out people well prepared for success in the 21st century. Although the aspirations for improvement are clearly humanistic – aimed at human betterment – the arguments offered in support of reform are almost entirely economic. A successful economy needs workers trained for jobs in existing and emerging industries; universities need revenues from grants, endowments and student tuition; and graduates need completed degrees to be successful in the job market.

This emphasis on economic outcomes to maintain the system in its present context risks falling dangerously short of what is needed for us to thrive in the operating conditions of the 21st century this book has described. The knowledge and capacities needed for the future will include traditional curricula that bring abstract knowledge and advanced technical skills. But unless this knowledge is held by people with well-developed personal capacities, anchored in particular cultural settings and understood holistically within a fully human framework, a 'muscle bound' emphasis on the logics of abstraction, reductionism and STEM (science, technology, engineering and maths) subjects may take us in entirely the wrong direction.

We would do better to follow elementary school teacher John Hunter (2011) who invented the World Peace Game in 1978 for his gifted 4th graders. Hunter is clearly a person of tomorrow, and it is the space that 'Mr Hunter' provides for his pupils that is transforming them, not the game.

He is pretty clear about that himself (in a typically humble way): "The World Peace Game is essentially an empty space. I like to think of it as a 21st-century wisdom table." He was thrown into teaching gifted children with no experience and had to follow his instincts: "There was no program directive, no manual to follow, no standards in gifted education... I endeavoured to clear a space for my students, an empty space, whereby they could create and make meaning out of their own understanding."

Hunter invites his pupils to engage with the full messiness of the world problematique. But they are not alone: "I throw them into this complex matrix, and they trust me because we have a deep, rich relationship together". That relationship and trust allow this remarkable teacher to be a different kind of leader: "I can't tell them anything because I don't know the answer. And I admit the truth to them right up front: I don't know. And because I don't know, they've got to dig up the answer."

It is encouraging that Hunter's TED talk about his work has gained such a following. It confirms the widespread yearning for true 21st-century education. Many creative young people today (who do not see a future in financial services or the big consulting firms) are seeking out alternative settings in which to grow and develop the competencies they know they will need in the century ahead.

Theirs is part of a wide-ranging search for relevant and affordable learning experiences for today's world. People are signing up for classes in transformation tools that they can then use with others, setting up their own social enterprises, learning in peer communities online and in flexible co-working spaces, travelling the world on the strength of social media connections, interning with inspiring organizations, seeking out mentors and fellow travellers.

In short, they are shifting the site of learning from formal education to what might be termed 'rehearsal spaces': places to work with groups or in experimental spaces that combine opportunities for experience, real encounters and guided reflection in a disciplined process – allowing people to develop and 'rehearse' their competence before demonstrating it 'in the real world'.

Rehearsal Spaces

This is in fact a well-established tradition. A central component in the history of the personal development movement has always been the group – or, more precisely, providing a set of conditions in which a group and its members can grow together in unpredictable and unique ways under disciplined guidance. It is a robust cultural template going back centuries.

One of the more influential initiatives of the post-war era was taken by Kurt Lewin, one of the founders of modern social psychology, who set up a research centre at MIT in 1944 exploring group dynamics. It was out of this work with community leaders and others that he developed the notion of action learning Training Groups or T-Groups – and in 1947 founded the National Training Laboratory for Group Development as a permanent centre.

There he ran facilitated dialogues to develop human relations through experiential, in-group settings away from the workplace. He described the Laboratory, set up in Bethel, Maine, as a 'cultural island' – where new group cultures could be explored. Lewin and others at NTL proved instrumental in establishing human relations as a legitimate field of study and practice in post-war management. The Tavistock Institute in the UK was an early follower.

By the 1960s, interest in 'cultural islands' where people could explore the further reaches of human potential had become much more widespread. Witness iconic places like Michael Murphy's Esalen, established on a beautiful headland in California as a dedicated site for personal growth and discovery – through guided group encounters of all kinds. It remains active to this day. Walt Anderson's *The Upstart Spring*, a wonderful history of Esalen, its triumphs, disasters, aspirations and its hubris, should be required reading for anyone seeking to enter this field today.

Aspects of that Esalen culture and its many and varied practices – from encounter, to gestalt, body work, meditation, yoga, expressive arts, psychodrama, martial arts, integral transformative practice and so on – are still very much available today. Residential encounter groups, for example, based on the same person-centred principles as those developed by Rogers and his colleagues decades ago, can still be found in many locations around the world – usually organized by independent local groups who see the value of such spaces for growth.

In our more anxious age however, these kinds of rehearsal spaces – safe, experimental spaces in which to try on other ways of being and relating – have tended to become more focused.

The most open are probably the 'learning journeys' originally brought to prominence in the practice of Global Business Network in the 1980s but now practised by many organizations, including IFF itself. These involve groups visiting a range of sites, looking around, meeting the people involved and then debriefing the experience. The sites are carefully chosen to challenge or expand existing views – usually around a present problem.

The participants might have watched videos or read case studies instead. But the learning journey offers (at least) three advantages: it deliberately includes visits to places with no immediate apparent relevance to the problem as currently framed; it immerses the participants in the lived reality of the cases rather than the abstract data; and it creates a shared experience within the group in which it becomes legitimate to notice that different people see and value different things. The guided reflection on such an experience can be immensely powerful: it is in the time for reflection that the moments of epiphany occur.

There are also now many organizations, and individuals, providing an extended setting, usually several days, to experiment with a particular tool, technique or process – evocative of the deeper competencies but also applicable in 'consulting' settings in the wider world.

A development of this approach is the 'Lab' – a form on the increase as our instinctive search for settings to support the expression of 21st-century competencies grows. This is an extension of the workshop format – providing an ongoing supported space for experiment in which people (often from very different fields) can come together for the purposes of discovery.

The model is the MIT Media Lab, established in 1985, which extended the idea of a scientist's laboratory into something more interdisciplinary and creative. In that case, technology is the medium, and smart products the output. But we can also see embedded in the Media Lab's philosophy many of the enabling conditions for developing the 21st-century competencies:

> *The Media Lab is a place where the future is lived, not imagined. Our domain is applying unorthodox research approaches for envisioning the impact of emerging technologies on everyday life.*
> *Unconstrained by traditional disciplines, Lab designers, engineers, artists, and scientists work atelier-style... Lab researchers foster a unique culture of learning by doing.*

The success of MIT Media Lab has spawned many imitators, including in areas other than technology. Often the discipline of design takes the coordinating place assigned to technology in the MIT model and the Lab morphs into a 'Studio'.

Ideally the Lab or the Studio is a physical space, although more often today the word is taken as a metaphor or a signifier for a particular style of working. Typically people will collaborate at a distance on a project, coming together from time to time for multi-day workshops – the whole process constituting a 'lab'. Adam Kahane's Reos Partners (2011), for example, offer a 'change lab' process to address complex challenges in any social system: "Depending on the challenge and the system, a change lab can be quick or extended, modest or ambitious, delimited or open-ended." Helsinki Design Lab, an offshoot of the Finnish Innovation Fund SITRA, offers a process of 'strategic design' and holds multi-day workshop sessions with its clients and partners that it calls 'studios'.

The language – lab, studio, design, innovation – is becoming interchangeable. The core concept remains the same: the provision of a protected space, supported in a disciplined way (by particularly skilled individuals, producers, or processes), in which people can collaborate and learn together outside the dominant culture. Properly designed and supported, these can become the rehearsal spaces for persons of tomorrow to find their voice, flex their 21st-century competencies, and develop the confidence to take them into the world.

This is precisely the context we have sought to create in our own programmes since the publication of the first edition of this book. We have also worked hard to develop a set of resources to support people in their working environments once they leave the rehearsal space and start playing for real. That includes the IFF Academy and the IFF Practice Centre, our international network of 'transformative innovators', and new books – *Three Horizons: The patterning of hope*, *Transformative Innovation: A guide to practice and policy* and *Braving Uncertainty: Living at the learning edge* – all of which provide more detail on the practice of expressing our 21st-century competencies in future-facing, culture-changing, inspirational and transformative action.[25]

CHAPTER 10:

PRACTICAL HOPE

Start Where You Are

If you have read this far, we assume it is because you appreciate the characteristics of the person of tomorrow, are attracted by the qualities of being, organizing and thinking that they display, are impressed by their capacity to get things done – including inspirational, culture-changing things – and are aware of the potential to develop further these same qualities in yourself.

The previous chapter explored the kinds of action that might both express your 21st-century competencies and develop them – messy, complex, hopeful, wise, patient, reflective, attuned to potential. It also offered some observations on the programmes, labs and other 'rehearsal spaces' available to help hone your awareness and tune up your competencies before getting into action for real.

This chapter will offer practical advice on this final step of taking on a real challenge, starting where you are. It is based on wide experience working in different contexts across the public, private and policy sectors, inside and outside formal organization.

But it is here that we encounter at full strength the paradox identified in Ed Schein's Foreword. We risk falling at last into the familiar pattern of the 'How-to' book – providing a glib recipe, a step-by-step process, an infallible guide for effective action and instant results.

As Schein notes, this is not that kind of book. Yet it is still a How-to book: "that asks nothing less of you than that you become a new person; a book that will enable you to understand and change what is going on and, in that process, will not only make you a better person, but enable you to make a better world."

In other words, even as we turn to doing, it is not all about doing. As we have said before, the first step is awareness. The capacity to read your landscape anew, to relish the life and vitality in complexity rather than become overwhelmed by it, is already a transformative stance. To bring your 21st-century self to work, consciously inhabiting your growing sense of being a person of tomorrow, will itself subtly shift the landscape and the culture around you. Remember Sun Tzu: we can win the battle without fighting. As our colleague Jim Ewing (2019) memorably put it: "to be a transformative presence is the highest form of our art".

Growing this sense of confidence in yourself and in those around you, developing and sustaining the quality of your presence, is a prerequisite for effective action and will itself have an impact. It will take time. And there will be setbacks. Don't rush it, and be ready to step back when you need to. This book is about dancing not *on* edge but *at* the edge. The edge is defined by the dance, by the point at which you are in danger of losing your balance. As you develop competence, so the edge will advance.

Our constant refrain about starting small should not therefore be read as lack of ambition. The Scottish writer Andrew Greig (2010) offers a wise perspective on scale: "There is no mountain in Scotland you cannot walk up and back down in a day, though that day might be long and the hill can be fatal. The Himalayas were awesome, astounding, possibly sublime, but I did not come to love them. They were too big to love; love implies some possible knowledge. But Suilven, Cul Mor, Canisp, Quinag, Glas Bheinn, are just the size to possess us. They rise above the human, without being entirely beyond us." You do not have to start by climbing Everest. Even if you do, you would be wise to take plenty of time to acclimatize as you go.

Our hope in any event is that with these resources, and with or without the additional experience of rehearsal, you will feel able to get started expressing your 21st-century competencies through effective, transformative action right where you are, in your existing organization, your community, your network, whatever pattern constitutes your working life, doing whatever it is you are doing, up against whatever it is that is sent to try you.

The long, slow process of adapting the institutions of 20th-century life to the demands of the complex present requires that people who have a sense of what the future needs work on that transformation from the inside. Cultural leadership in our view is an inside job, not something developed elsewhere and transplanted wholesale. It can start small, but the more you do it the better you get at it, and the more you change the culture you are in, the more the culture around you will change.

Hence the rest of this chapter offers some initial guidance on how to put the contents of this book into practice where you are now, in your present setting or organization. The IFF Practice Centre contains resources to help.

Inspiration

As you have read through this book you have probably been thinking about your own circle. Do you know anyone who seems to be coping with the demands of the 21st century better than most? Someone seemingly more at home in the confusion, effective in action, not overwhelmed? Someone who seems to have it all together? Chances are that you do.

In numerous workshops now we have asked that question and invited participants to identify the qualities of being, being together, knowing and doing that they observe in such persons. The results, across different cultures and different demographics, are remarkably similar – compassion, humility, energy, empathy, rigour, openness, care, persistence and so on. Try it yourself now.

What the exercise also brings to awareness is the presence of these qualities in ourselves. Maybe not all of them to the same extent: it is impossible to think of anyone who excels across the full profile (which is another reason why we cannot be competent alone). But these are very evident human characteristics, not beyond us.

Secondly, although they might have to start out with celebrities or public figures, or even with imaginary individuals ('if there were such a person, what characteristics would they display?'), most people can identify one or two people in their immediate circle who are already exhibiting 21st-century competence to some degree.

You can do that too. Think about your network in relation to the qualities of being, being together, knowing and doing that you have identified as fitting for the 21st century. Who is demonstrating something that you admire and feel you could develop yourself? Think about approaching that person and asking whether they would be willing to be a sounding board for you, a conversation partner, to support your developmental journey. You may be surprised – if you really have found a person of tomorrow their support could be very significant.

In the absence of such an individual – indeed as a complement in any event – it will be helpful to have materials to hand to help you reflect on your experience and inform the path you develop for yourself. This book and its references will be useful – especially Part Two on the ways of being, organizing, knowing and doing exhibited by persons of tomorrow. It does no harm to become a voracious reader, always remembering the old adage that 'if you want a new idea read an old book'.

Ultimately you are going to have to try something novel in the context of your existing working environment: start where you are.

Prompts

The first step might be to get hold of a set of IFF Prompt Cards – or download the app. This is a collection of statements derived from IFF's practical work, each intended to prompt a shift out of familiar patterns of being, perceiving, thinking, framing towards something more capacious and in line with the thrust of this book. They are about learning, direction, integrity, perception – "Recognize the different value patterns", "Perception first, then analysis", "Tolerate differences in order to discover richer wholeness" and so on. They effectively encapsulate a whole curriculum, reminding us of the 21st-century competencies and how to embody them.

These prompts can be used as conversation starters, or to stimulate new ideas when you get stuck. Some people take a card a day and seek to embody it – as a disciplined practice in competence development. As cards they lend themselves to all kinds of games: there is a particularly popular 'tarot' reading, and a game called 'strategy poker'. But above all they offer a simple reminder – a timely prompt – of ways of knowing, being, doing and being together that we already possess but need to be encouraged to bring to the surface.

A second resource is Kitbag, already mentioned earlier in Chapter 6 – a specially designed set of resources to develop inner strength and psychological stamina, to remain the artist of your own life in a pattern of other lives rather than becoming overwhelmed by complexity.

Like the prompt cards, Kitbag can be used either by an individual or – more powerfully – in groups. Its elements deliberately seek to evoke and develop inner resources, accessed through a science of qualities rather than quantities. This too can be used as a practice – daily, weekly, monthly. Just choose the elements that work best for you.

In many organizational settings both the prompt cards and Kitbag will feel counter-cultural. Thus it can be a useful first move in trying out your 21st-century competence and your skill in reading the culture to introduce these into your work setting. Think carefully about how to calibrate this 'small act of creative transgression'. Do not invite resistance. Start small.

You might simply draw a prompt card to open or close a meeting. Or invite everyone to do so if a meeting runs into trouble – to see what new perspectives show up. Take one element from the Kitbag and use it for the check-in. Or suggest the meeting just 'takes a minute' to gather itself before launching on its agenda (there is a one-minute timer in Kitbag, and a set of 'presence cards' suggesting how best to spend a minute to maintain competence in the face of stress).

What we are testing here is the art of introducing the new in the presence of the old. Our colleague Neville Singh advises 'tact, timing and titration': be tactful and respectful by not introducing your initiative as critical of the existing culture or making it wrong; choose the right moment for your small act of creative transgression; and when you do, calibrate it artfully, choose the right dose, don't push too far too fast.

Form A Creative Integrity

Perhaps these small 'transgressions' will attract interest or intrigue from colleagues. You will gain a sense of who else might be interested in 21st-century competencies. This gives you the opening for the next step: form a creative integrity.

We will not dissemble here. This is a big step and not an easy task. This is where the suggestions about action in the previous chapter come into play. You need to identify an important challenge, find some colleagues up for addressing it with you, and establish a creative integrity to take it on.

With your small team in place (no solo climbers), consider the four poles of the integrity model:

Sovereignty: what resources do you need? A place to meet? Somebody to provide the sandwiches? A small travel budget, e.g. for learning journeys? And so on. Again this will start small – but the question of sovereignty or the control of resources (broadly defined) will be something to return to over time as the creative integrity develops, and particularly as it gets into action and begins to write its own history.

Recognition: how public do you want to be? Are you going to give yourselves a name or an identity? Do you need support from a senior colleague or mentor? Likewise, these questions are likely to become more pressing as you become more visible. The support of a senior colleague can be doubly valuable at that stage: to legitimize actions that may seem counter-cultural to others, and to capitalize on the learning and results for the wider system when you are successful.

Reciprocity: do you need to establish cordial, mutually supportive relationships with others – individuals or institutions? That might apply particularly to relationships between members of the initial integrity and their host divisions or organizations. Are there resources you lack that might become available through reciprocity? Are you ready to acknowledge reciprocity as a guiding principle within the creative integrity itself: i.e. all for one and one for all, nobody in charge, shared responsibility, etc.? The reciprocity question will need revisiting as the integrity becomes more visible. There may be some delicate internal politics to deal with – another chance to test the 21st-century competencies.

Agency: in a way, paying attention to the other poles will take care of this one. But it does remind us that in order to develop competence we have to take action. All four poles will need to be revisited as the journey progresses: your actions will impact how you are seen, the resources you can command and the relationships you develop. Even at the outset, once you have decided on an action quickly check back against the other domains – sovereignty, recognition, reciprocity – to see whether they are adequately resourced to support the agency you intend.

Reflect and Learn

At this point the integrity transforms into an action learning setting in which each member becomes coach to the others. As noted in the previous chapter, maintaining a regular schedule of meetings for the purpose of reflection through the development of a project is useful. It becomes part of the discipline.

It is good to have a protocol for such sessions – so that they are genuinely self-organizing and operate in tune with the integrity. We have found in our own programmes that an initial check-in round with each person drawing an IFF prompt card and reflecting on what it has to say to them in the context of the development of the project is a good opener. It may be that you want to go further and incorporate elements from the IFF Kitbag to emphasize being together at a human level. These practices can be explicitly about developing capacity within the group – which could itself be a topic for reflection in other sessions.

A protocol about equal time for each participant to be the centre of coaching attention is useful and in keeping with the notion of reciprocity. And it helps to maintain the coaching stance (without specialist training or facilitation for that purpose) if those providing support are allowed only to ask questions, not give advice. Better still if the person being coached then gets to answer in the session itself only the questions they want to, holding the others for longer term reflection. The questions should be open (i.e. not 'yes/no') and framed to generate insight rather than for information.

It helps to maintain the integrity of the action learning process if the focus in these sessions is always a reflection on results – what happened? what didn't happen? how well did it go? That maintains the momentum of a real learning cycle balancing action and reflection. But do spend time at the end of each session reflecting as a group on what you are discovering about developing and putting into practice the 21st-century competencies.

Action learning, deploying the 21st-century competencies, will generate remarkable results. It is the accumulation of these effective acts of creative transgression, each initiated by small and slowly expanding creative integrities, that will gradually shift the culture – and the performance – of the whole organization.

Never Forget the Bigger Game

This approach likely sounds familiar. It is not unusual to have organizations establish explicit spaces and places for counter-cultural activity. There is no shortage of skunk works and innovation labs. 'Google time', in which employees get the freedom to devote 20% of their work time to 'whatever they think will most benefit Google', is a popular concept – although insiders (some of whom think of it as 120% Google time) suggest it is more a symbolic signal of creative freedom than a hard and fast rule.

Whatever the means for carving out space for something new, the difference in what we are proposing here is also about ends – the nature of the intention. 'Innovation' is a neutral term – it can apply equally to fixing the existing system, incrementally improving it, or just disrupting it to see what happens. But persons of tomorrow, operating in integrity, and consciously as part of a human system, are usually only peripherally interested in this kind of innovation. As described in the previous chapter, 'wise initiative and practical hope' for them is not just different but transformative. It is values based, contributing towards greater wholeness, and with its eye on the long term.

Where labs, skunk works or Google time already exist in an organization they can provide powerful enabling conditions for pursuing, and scaling, the kind of work we describe. But they do not provide, in themselves, the settings required for growing the 21st-century competencies. As we suggest, those must be more intentionally designed.

Persons of tomorrow are consciously part of a much larger story of change. Innovation per se and the pursuit of the new, new thing is meaningless. We are engaged in a bigger game, always played out locally and in context but on a global stage. We are hospice workers to the dying culture and midwives to the new.

CHAPTER 11:

CONCLUSION

Why Last Chapters Disappoint

It is traditional for books like this to conclude with a final chapter offering a call to action, a blueprint for how to put the preceding analysis into practice at scale and to transform the world in the process. Yet it is also at this point that many books seeking to address complex social, cultural or political issues let us down.

David Greenberg (2011) provides numerous examples in a New York Times essay on 'Why Last Chapters Disappoint'. He suggests this is partly a consequence of the sheer complexity of the problems they deal with and the difficulty therefore in coming up with 'solutions' that are not either 'blindingly obvious' or else hopelessly impractical or utopian. Yet the culture today seems to demand that anybody reflecting on a complex circumstance is obliged at the same time to suggest a comprehensive response. Greenberg quotes H L Mencken making the same point as long ago as 1926: "To lack a remedy is to lack the very license to discuss disease".

We hope we have avoided the danger in this case since in a way the majority of this book is about response. The early chapters detail our view of the changing context, the consequences mounting worldwide of our inadequate responses to date (both in the physical world and in our human system), and the need to pay attention therefore to developing 21st-century competencies individually and in groups, organizations and cultures, in order to become effective again as authors of our own future.

The second part of the book focuses on how to do this in practice. We have taken the framework developed in the Delors Commission report and have considered it in the context of the 21st century, learning how to be, how to be together, how to know and how to do. And across the board the focus has been on persons, living in relationship with others, seeking hope, meaning and purpose in their own lives while inevitably operating in organizational and cultural settings that cannot be ignored and that need to learn and grow alongside them.

Blowing an Uncertain Trumpet

In a way we have also conceived this book as a final chapter in itself. In 2005 our friend and colleague Eamonn Kelly, CEO of Global Business Network, wrote a wonderful book called *Powerful Times: Rising to the challenge of our uncertain future*. After decades of experience working with diverse clients to explore scenarios for the future, Kelly took some time out to consider what all of this work might be telling us about the future we can expect.

His conclusion was that for every plausible, evidence-based story about the way the world is going there is an opposite, equally plausible, evidence-based story. Instead of a coherent trajectory into the future he identified a host of 'dynamic tensions' pulling the world in opposite directions (prosperity and decline, for example, technology acceleration and pushback, clarity and craziness). Hence the title of his book – a reference to Pandolfo Petrucci's response to Machiavelli when investigated for his inconstant and confusing behaviour: "Wishing to make as few mistakes as possible, I arrange my affairs hour by hour, because the times are more powerful than our brains."

Implicit in Petrucci's statement, and in Kelly's book, is a call to develop new competencies and capacities (not just in our brains) to meet the challenges of the times. There are hints throughout the text at what such capacities might be, nowhere more so than in the final chapter on how "three important sets of actors – businesses, leaders and global citizens – will be largely responsible for shaping a better future." Yet it left us wanting more: both a more explicit examination of the 21st-century competencies required and how we might develop them in practice.

This book is one result of that quest. But it is also no more than the tip of an iceberg – reflecting on decades of experience and our own evolving practice. We are not describing in these pages simply a set of desirables for what should be, but rather a new cultural frame that reveals more of what is: the wealth and potential of persons of tomorrow already in our midst and within our own capacity to develop.

Our own work has become increasingly attuned therefore to the identification of 21st-century competencies in practice and the design of the support structures, the mentoring, the organizational settings, the enabling conditions to help them grow. While much of what we have learned is distilled in Part Two, there is much more that can be said. Each chapter should be seen as an introduction to further exploration and more specific resources. How to bring 21st-century competencies to healthcare, for example, or education, or enterprise. And so on. Already we are in touch with a healthy and growing community of practice developing and expressing 21st-century competencies in diverse settings. We encourage readers of this book to join. As we have said many times, 21st-century competencies are not developed alone.

We issue the invitation as aspirant persons of tomorrow ourselves. We offer the message of this book therefore with all due humility, but not a little passion. The consequences of living in powerful times with inadequate cultures to support us are manifest and ever more pressing. At the same time the market for quick fixes, false hope, silver bullets and 'the smack of firm leadership' is booming. To borrow the words of Theodore Hesburgh, Catholic priest and long-time President of the University of Notre Dame, leadership in such a culture demands certainty: "You cannot blow an uncertain trumpet."

On the contrary. Today's times require a more nuanced response – based on the stance outlined in Chapter 5: humility, balance and a faith in the future. We must become virtuosos in playing the uncertain trumpet. Perhaps in time we will achieve the degree of mastery described by the Sufi musician and mystic Hazarat Inayat Khan. He saw harmony as a greater virtue than truth and hoped in time to "sound a note so deep as to embrace all humanity."

We hope our own initial attempts to give voice to the theme of 'persons of tomorrow' will at least find some wider resonance in the culture. Like Rogers himself we fully anticipate that others will come to "flesh these ideas out more fully" in the future. So we see the end of this chapter not as a full stop, but a semi-colon. Cultures change slowly, and they change through conversation.

So let's give the last word to Rogers (1980), who says:

> *If the time comes when our culture tires of endless homicidal feuds, despairs of the use of force and war as a means of bringing peace, becomes discontent with the half lives its members are living, only then will our culture seriously look for alternatives. And when they do, they will not find a void... They will realize that there are ways, already tried out on a small scale, of enhancing learning, of moving towards new values, of raising consciousness to new levels.*

We offer this book as a contribution to this process, certainly not as a conclusion.

References

American Psychiatric Association (1980) *Diagnostic and Statistical Manual of Mental Disorders.* (3rd ed., text rev.) American Psychiatric Association

Anderson, W. T. (1979) *Open Secrets: A western guide to Tibetan Buddhism.* Viking

_____ (1983) *The Upstart Spring: Esalen and the human potential movement: the first twenty years.* iUniverse

Antonovsky, A. (1996) 'The salutogenic model as a theory to guide health promotion'. *Health Promotion International,* Vol 11, No 1

Ariely, D. (2008) *Predictably Irrational: The hidden forces that shape our decisions.* HarperCollins

Bateson, G. (1972) *Steps to an Ecology of Mind.* Jason Aronson

Bauman, Z. (2010) *Letters from the Liquid Modern World.* Polity Press

Bellah, R. N., Madsen, R., Sullivan, W. M., & Tipton, S. M. (1985) *Habits of the Heart: Individualism and commitment in American life.* Harper and Row

Blom, P. (2008) *The Vertigo Years: Change and culture in the West, 1900-1914.* Basic Books

Bohm, D. (1980) *Wholeness and the Implicate Order.* Routledge

Boisot, Max *et al.* (2011) *Collisions and Collaboration: The organization of learning in the ATLAS Experiment at the LHC.* Oxford University Press

Boyer, D., Cook, J. W. & Steinberg, M. (2010) *In Studio: Recipes for systemic change.* Sitra

Bridger, H. (1990) 'Courses and working conferences as transitional learning institutions'. In E. Trist & H. Murray (Eds.), *The Social Engagement of Social Science: A Tavistock anthology (Vol. 1)* University of Pennsylvania Press

Brinn, L. (Producer), & Duckworth, M. (Director) (2008) 'What is behavioral economics, and where are the free lunches?' Duke University – Fuqua School of Business. [Video File] Retrieved from http://bit.ly/TPpt01

Broadbent, S. (24 July, 2006) 'Ask not for whom the bell tolls'. *The Guardian*. Retrieved from http://bit.ly/TPpt2

Broadie, A. (2001) *The Scottish Enlightenment: The historical age of the historical nation*. Birlinn

Brueggemann, W. (2001) *The Prophetic Imagination*. 2nd ed. Fortress Press

Bumiller, E. (26 April, 2010) 'We have met the enemy and he is PowerPoint'. *The New York Times* (p. A1)

Collins, A. *et al.* (1991) 'Cognitive apprenticeship: Making things visible'. *American Educator: The Professional Journal of the American Federation of Teachers*, 15(3), 6-11,38-46

Collins, J. (2001) *Good to Great*. Harper Business

Csikszentmihalyi, M. (1993) *The Evolving Self: A psychology for the third millennium*. Harper Perennial

de Bono, E. (1985) *Six Thinking Hats: An essential approach to business management*. Little, Brown & Co

Delors, J., Al Mufti, I., Amagi, I., Carneiro, R., Chung, F. *et al.* (1996) *Learning: The treasure within. Report to UNESCO of the International Commission on Education for the Twenty-First Century*. UNESCO Publishing

Dods, R. & Andrews, N. (2010) 'The people theme: Thriving in the 21st century: Competencies, qualities and attributes for the arts & cultural sector in times of complexity, change and uncertainty'. Retrieved from http://bit.ly/TPpt03

Drucker, P. (1993) *Post-Capitalist Society*. HarperCollins

Dyer, G. (2008) *Climate Wars*. Random House Canada

Dyson, F. (22 December, 2011) 'How to dispel your illusions'. *New York Review of Books*. Retrieved from http://bit.ly/TPpt04

Eckersley, R. (2004) 'New world view struggles to emerge'. *The Futurist*; Sep/Oct 2004; 38, 5

Ewing, J. (2019) *Braving Uncertainty: Living at the learning edge*. Triarchy Press

Fairtlough, G. (2007) *The Three Ways of Getting Things Done: Hierarchy, heterarchy and responsible autonomy in organizations.* Triarchy Press

Festinger, L. (1957) *A Theory of Cognitive Dissonance.* Stanford University Press

Frankl, V. (1959) *Man's Search for Meaning.* Beacon Press

Freire, P. (1998) *Pedagogy of Freedom: Ethics, democracy, and civic courage.* Rowman & Littlefield

Freud, S. (1930/2002) *Civilization and its Discontents.* Penguin

Friedman, T. (12 July, 2011) 'The start-up of you'. *The New York Times*, (p. A27)

Füssel, S. (2003) *Gutenberg and the Impact of Printing.* Ashgate

Gardner, H. (1983) *Frames of Mind: The theory of multiple intelligences.* Basic Books

Gawande, A. (2009) *The Checklist Manifesto: How to get things right.* Picador

Greenberg, D. (18 March, 2011) 'Why Last Chapters Disappoint'. *The New York Times*

Greenspan, E., ed. (2005) *Walt Whitman's 'Song of Myself': A sourcebook and critical edition.* Routledge

Greig, A. (2010) *At the Loch of the Green Corrie.* Riverrun

Halliwell, E., Main L. & Richardson, C. (2007) *The Fundamental Facts.* Mental Health Foundation

Hayward, T. (May 18, 2010) Interview with Sky News television

Held, B. (2010) 'Why is there universality in rationality?' *Journal of Theoretical and Philosophical Psychology*, 30(1), 1-16

Hess, E.D. & Ludwig, K. (2017) *Humility is the New Smart.* Berrett-Koehler

Hirschman, A. (1991) *The Rhetoric of Reaction: Perversity, futility, jeopardy.* The Belknap Press of Harvard University Press

Hunter, J. (March 2011) *John Hunter: Teaching with the World Peace Game.* [Video File] retrieved from http://bit.ly/TPpt05

Huntington, S.P (1996). *The Clash of Civilizations and the Remaking of World Order.* Touchstone

Hyde, L. (2008) *Trickster makes this world: How disruptive imagination creates culture.* Canongate Books

Institute of Directors (1994) *Good Practice for Boards of Directors (An Investigation into Standards in UK Companies by the Institute of Directors, sponsored by the Training, Education and Enterprise Directorate of the Department of Employment, and carried out by Henley Management College).* HMSO

Jackson Lears, T. J. (1994) *No Place of Grace: Antimodernism and the transformation of American culture, 1880-1920.* University of Chicago Press

James, W. (1902) *Varieties of Religious Experience.* Penguin

_____ (1907) 'The energies of men'. *The Philosophical Review*, XVI(1), 1-20

Jobs, S. (June 12, 2005) Commencement address. Stanford University, Palo Alto, CA

Jullien, F. (2004) *A Treatise on Efficacy: Between Western and Chinese thinking.* University of Hawaii Press

Kahneman, D. (2011) *Thinking Fast and Slow.* Farrer, Straus and Giroux

Kay, J. (2010) *Obliquity: Why our goals are best achieved indirectly.* Profile Books

Kegan, R. & Lahey, L. L. (2009) *Immunity to Change.* Harvard Business School Press

Kegan, R. (1994) *In Over Our Heads: The mental demands of modern life.* Harvard University Press

Kelly, E. (2005) *Powerful Times: Rising to the challenge of our uncertain world.* Pearson Prentice Hall

Koestler, A. (1967) *The Ghost in the Machine.* Random House

Konrath, S., O'Brien, E. & Hsing, C. (2011) 'Changes in dispositional empathy in American college students over time: A meta-analysis'. *Personality and Social Psychology Review*, 15(2), 180-198

Kurtz, H. (13 January, 2011) 'Obama's next impossible speech'. *The Daily Beast.* Retrieved 2012-07-23. http://bit.ly/TPpt06

Laing, R. D. (1971) *Knots.* Penguin

Lear, J. (2006) *Radical Hope: Ethics in the face of cultural devastation.* Harvard University Press

Leicester, G. H. (2007) *Rising to the Occasion: Cultural leadership in powerful times.* Mission Models Money, UK. Available at http://bit.ly/TPpt07

_____ (2014) *The Producer Role and the Art of the Impossible: A reflection on the practice of Helen Marriage, Artichoke.* International Futures Forum

_____ (2016) *Transformative Innovation: A guide to practice and policy.* Triarchy Press

Leicester, G. H. and O'Hara, M. (2007) *Ten Things to Do in a Conceptual Emergency.* Triarchy Press

Levi, R. (2003) *Group Magic: An inquiry into experiences of collective resonance.* Doctoral Dissertation – Executive Summary. Retrieved from http://bit.ly/TPpt08

Linskey, A. (May 23, 2019) 'Obama without Obama-ism: 2020 Democrats embrace the ex-president but not his policies', *Washington Post*

Little, R. (August 18, 2011) Keynote speech for Arts Council England & Festivals Edinburgh Talent Symposium 2011 'Stewardship, connections and ecology: contexts for the development of talent'. http://bit.ly/TPpt09 (accessed 27 August 2012)

Lockwood, D. (2011) *The Islamic Republic of Dewsbury.* The Press News

Loy, D. (1988) *Non-Duality: A study in comparative philosophy.* Humanity Books

Maslow, A. (1970) *Motivation and Personality* (2nd ed.) Harper & Row

_____ (1962) *Towards a Psychology of Being.* Insight Van Nostrand

May, R. (1983) *The Discovery of Being: Writings in existential psychology.* W. W. Norton

McChrystal, S. (2009) COMISAF's Initial Assessment. Secretary of Defense Memorandum 26 June 2009. http://bit.ly/TPpt10 (accessed 29 August, 2012)

McCracken, G. (2008) *Transformations: Identity construction in contemporary culture.* Indiana University Press

McLuhan, T. C. (1972) *Touch the Earth: A self-portrait of Indian existence.* Pocket Books

Meadows, D. H., Meadows, D. L. Randers, J. and Behrens III, W. (1972) *The Limits to Growth.* Universe Books

Michael, D. (1973a) *On Learning to Plan and Planning to Learn.* Jossey-Bass

_____ (1973b) 'Technology and the management of change from the perspective of a culture context'. *Technological Forecasting and Social Change,* 5, 219-232

_____ (2010) *In Search of the Missing Elephant: Selected essays,* Triarchy Press

Mintzberg, H. (1979) *The Structuring of Organizations.* Prentice Hall

Mitroff, I. (2005) *Why Some Companies Emerge Stronger and Better from a Crisis.* AMACOM

NCES (National Center for Education Statistics) (2009) *The Condition of Education 2009* (NCES 2009-081)

Nussbaum, M. (2001) *Upheavals of Thought: The intelligence of emotions.* Cambridge University Press

O'Hara, M. (2009) 'Another inconvenient truth and the developmental role for psychology in a threatened world'. *The Humanistic Psychologist,* 38(2), 101-119

_____ (2011, March) 'Generation Open: The future of higher education in a DIY world'. E-forum: culture and consciousness, Retrieved from http://bit.ly/TPpt11

OECD (Organization for Economic Co-operation and Development) (2003) *Key Competencies for a Successful Life and a Well-Functioning Society* (ed. Rychen D.S. & Salganik L.H.), Hogrefe & Huber

Omer, A. (2005) 'The Spacious Center: Leadership and the creative transformation of culture', *Shift,* March-May 2005

Orlov, D. (2008) *Reinventing Collapse.* New Society Books

Postman, N. (1985) *Amusing Ourselves to Death: Public discourse in the age of show business.* Penguin

Ramachandran, V. S. (2011) *The Tell-Tale Brain.* W. W. Norton

Rayner, S. (2007) 'The rise of risk and the decline of politics'. *Environmental Hazards,* 7 (2) 165-172

Reos Partners. (2011) *Change Labs.* Retrieved from http://bit.ly/TPpt16

Rogers, C. R. (1980) *A Way of Being.* Houghton Mifflin

Roszak, T. (1969) *The Making of a Counter-Culture.* Doubleday

Scott, J. C. (1999) *Seeing like a State: How certain schemes to improve the human condition have failed.* Yale University Press

Schein, E. H. (1992) *Organizational Culture and Leadership.* Jossey Bass

Schein, E. H. & Schein, P. A. (2018) *Humble leadership: The power of relationships, openness and trust.* Berrett-Koehler.

_____ (2019) *The Corporate Culture Survival Guide,* 3rd ed, Wiley

Schön, D. A. (1983) *The Reflective Practitioner: How professionals think in action.* Basic Books

Schwartz, P., Leyden P. & Hyatt J. (1999) *The Long Boom.* Basic Books

Segal, D. (May 1, 2010) 'It's complicated: Making sense of complexity'. *The New York Times*

Senge, P. M. (1990) *The Fifth Discipline: The art and practice of the learning organization.* Doubleday

Sennett, R. (2006) *The Culture of the New Capitalism.* Yale University Press

Sharpe, W. (2010) *Economies of Life: Patterns of health and wealth.* Triarchy Press

_____ (2013) *Three Horizons: The patterning of hope.* Triarchy Press

Shipp, E. R. (October 25, 2005) 'Rosa Parks, 92, founding symbol of civil rights movement, dies'. *The New York Times*

Shweder, R. A. (1991) *Thinking Through Cultures: Expeditions in cultural psychology.* Harvard University Press

Shweder, R. A. & Bourne, E. (1982) 'Does the concept of the person vary cross-culturally?' In A. J. Marsella & G. White, *Cultural Concepts in Mental Health and Therapy,* pp. 97-137

Smith, Z. (February 26, 2009) 'Speaking in tongues'. *New York*

Review of Books. Retrieved from http://bit.ly/TPpt12

Staudinger, U. M., Dörner, J., & Mickler, C. (2005) 'Wisdom and personality' in *A Handbook of Wisdom: Psychological perspectives*, R. J. Sternberg & J. Jordan, (Eds.) Cambridge University Press

Stern, S. (November 10, 2006) 'Leadership: Industry maps DNA of 21st- century movers and shakers'. *Financial Times*

Sunstein, C., & Thaler, R. (2008) *Nudge: Improving decisions about health, wealth and happiness.* Yale University Press

Tawil, S. & Cougoureux, M. (2013) *Revisiting Learning: the treasure within.* UNESCO Educational Research and Foresight-Occasional paper. http://bit.ly/TPpt18

Tyndall, K. (2007) *The Producers: Alchemists of the impossible.* Arts Council England and The Jerwood Charitable Foundation

Universal Declaration of Human Rights, G.A. res. 217A (III), U.N. Doc A=810 at 71 (1948)

Vickers, G. (1983) *Human Systems are Different.* Sage Publications

Watts, A. (1961) *Psychotherapy East and West.* Random House

Wyer, R. S., Chiu, C-y., Hong, Y.-y. (Eds.) (2009) *Understanding Culture: Theory, research and application.* Psychology Press

Yankelovich, D. (1991) *Coming to Public Judgment: Making democracy work in a complex world.* Syracuse University Press

Yeats, W. B. (1920/1998) 'The Second Coming' in Harmon, W. (ed) *The Classic Hundred Poems.* Columbia University Press

Zielenziger, M. (2006) *Shutting Out the Sun: How Japan created its own lost generation.* Nan A. Talese

Notes

1 See (Leicester & O'Hara, 2007) and the related website: www.conceptualemergency.com

2 (OECD, 2003) – materials from which can be viewed at http://deseco.ch – defines 'competence' and yet uses throughout the plural form 'competencies' (rather than competences). We have adopted the same pattern in spite of its inconsistency. We do so because we feel that 'competence' is a more natural singular term than 'competency' for our purposes, since it feels more capacious, less technical and more suited to our purposes given that we are always talking about attributes of whole persons. 'Competencies' feels like the natural plural. We have at least tried to be consistent in sticking to this formulation throughout the book and hope the result is not confusing.

3 The term 'persons of tomorrow' is partly chosen because it recognises Rogers' earlier insight that becoming a 'person' is itself an achievement, locating one's individual self as inevitably in relationship with others.

4 We are drawing on the work of our IFF colleague Aftab Omer, President of Meridian University, California for the theoretical framework that advances the idea of creative transgression as lying at the heart of cultural leadership. In his 2005 paper on The Spacious Center, which has been very influential on our thinking, Omer further suggests that "creative transgressions are a specific kind of creative action characterized by three distinct features. First, they involve principled actions. Second, they involve imaginative actions. Third, they entail conscious sacrifice." As will be clear from the examples of small acts of cultural leadership we have chosen to highlight later in the book, we believe it is wise to calibrate these features to suit our specific circumstances.

5 Some will question whether Aung San Suu Kyi should still feature in this list of exceptional political leaders from the first edition of the book. She has endured a very public fall from grace since her election as de facto head of government in Myanmar in November 2015. Perhaps she has revealed 'feet of clay' – a danger we highlight on page 26. Equally, the context in which she is operating, as head of government, is very different from that in which she rose to prominence – campaigning for democracy in a military dictatorship, largely whilst under some form of detention over twenty years. The changed context has brought a need to adapt where previously her constancy was her strength.

6 A resolution passed at the Sixty-Fifth World Health Assembly (WHA65) of the World Health Organization in May 2012 states that 13% of the world's burden of disease and 23-35% of all years spent living with a disability are from mental disorders.

7 Jim Collins (2001) cleverly made a virtue out of this with his subsequent volume, *How the Mighty Fall*.

8 See Kelly (2005). The book opens with a tale of intrigue in Renaissance Italy when Machiavelli was sent from Florence to investigate the erratic behaviour of Pandolfo Petrucci, the Lord of neighbouring Siena. Machiavelli was impressed by Petrucci's explanation: "Wishing to make as few mistakes as possible, I conduct my government day by day and arrange my affairs hour by hour, because the times are more powerful than our brains."

9 There is no word in English that can accommodate collectively the diverse elements that affect human minds. This led Maureen O'Hara to invent 'psychosphere'. Analogous to 'ecosphere', it refers to the holistic "interconnected, interpenetrated mutually influential system of narratives, symbols, images, representations, languages, metaphors, patterns of life, values, epistemologies, cognitive habits, rituals, religions, power relationships, sports, forms of commerce, governance, metaphysics, art, and technologies" that delineates the psychological context of individual and group life (O'Hara, 2009) .

10 Psychospheres large and small produce distinct mentalities that are held stable by vast webs of mutually reinforcing physical,

environmental and relational social patterning. The burgeoning field of cultural psychology reveals variations in basic mental functions such as perception, category formation, motivation, sense of justice, neurological development, learning and meta-cognitive conceptual ordering which result in different ways of thinking and acting. Many authors have shown that the Western mentality differs from the Eastern one along several important dimensions and these differences are learned (Wyer, Chiu & Hong, 2009). The mental life of pre-industrial people is considerably different from that of people raised in societies that have developed advanced technologies (Shweder & Bourne, 1982). In *Seeing like a State*, Scott (1999) describes a mentality that uses economic ideas and values and relies heavily on statistical reasoning which emerged in 17th-century Europe. He points out that this way of looking at the world is held together by power structures, values, economic systems and administrative protocols which make sense within societies with centralized power structures and has become the conventional wisdom of modernity. Edgar Schein (1992) has described organizational cultures (and even subcultures among the different operational groups like the engineers and HR professionals within a single company) that support ways of being and doing and create blind spots and dysfunctions particular to that company. When important sustaining structures are disrupted, as they are in a war or long occupation, or people stop subscribing to them as when the Berlin Wall came down, mentalities can collapse. Often with great turbulence and distress.

11 'Western culture' here might equally be called 'Modernity' – the world view that emerged in Europe during the 15th century and has dominated its values, social identity and civic life since then.

12 In using this phrase, Jobs was himself referring back to one of the products of the cultural openness of the 1960s, the Whole Earth Catalog launched by Stewart Brand in 1968 and which published its final edition in 1974. Jobs was thus explicitly linking his message to the next generation to the spirit of cultural renewal of forty years previously. As he put it: "On the back cover of their final issue was a photograph of an early morning country road, the kind you might find yourself hitchhiking on if you were so

adventurous. Beneath it were the words: "Stay Hungry. Stay Foolish." It was their farewell message as they signed off. "Stay Hungry. Stay Foolish." And I have always wished that for myself. And now, as you graduate anew, I wish that for you." The full archive of the Catalog, including this famous back cover, is available at http://bit.ly/TPpt14

13 Staudinger *et al.* (2005) suggest that studies that look at wisdom as an individual quality might be under-reporting the distribution of wisdom in the population however. When experimental conditions are changed and participants are allowed to bring a person with them to the lab whom they trust and usually rely on to talk over difficult issues, wisdom scores increase and as many as one in five people give wise responses. This has led some researchers to speculate that given the right combination of general intelligence, personality integration and balance of altruism and individualism and a social context where tacit knowledge can be prompted, wisdom might be a more common human resource than we realize.

14 For a report compiling official statistics on the incidence of mental disorders see Halliwell *et al.* (2007). They report that, in any one year, "1 in 4 British adults experience at least one mental disorder" and "approximately 450 million people worldwide have a mental health problem" p.7. The Mental Health Foundation also report self-harm statistics are the highest in Europe, and Scottish suicide rates are twice those in the rest of the UK.

15 Quoted in a 2012 interview in *Time.*

16 In 1966, in the opening sentences of *The Psychology of Science*, Maslow made public his epistemological challenge to conventional Western psychology. "This book", he stated, "is not an argument within orthodox science; it is a critique (à la Gödel) of orthodox science and of the ground on which it rests". Joined and influenced by such seminal thinkers as Ludwig von Bertalanffy, Gregory Bateson, Michael Polanyi, Jacob Bronowski, Aldous Huxley, Carl Rogers, and Thomas Kuhn as well as his own studies of Eastern thought, Maslow set out to redefine psychology as a holistic science of Being that would include

human experience from the depths of the inner world to the social worlds of human societies and to the outer reaches of evolving consciousness.

17 Management expert and psychologist Ian Mitroff, for example, has found in a series of interviews conducted across the corporate world in the U.S. that: "First... people desperately want an opportunity to realize their potential as whole human beings, both on and off the job. Second they want to work for ethical organizations. Third, they want to do interesting work. And while making money certainly is important, at best it is a distant fourth goal for most people." This and other evidence of the search for meaning and personal development through work is to be found in Leicester (2007).

18 This reach towards a more holistic integration of being and doing can be seen in events such as the Burning Man festival in the Nevada desert, Open Space conference design, once counter-cultural but now used by mainstream organizations to design conferences that go beyond talking heads and the SOCAP (Social Capital) events where financial viability, business models and spiritual practices are considered on the same panels.

19 McChrystal was dismissed by President Obama less than a year later after an article in *Rolling Stone* magazine in which he and his staff were recorded criticizing administration officials.

20 In order not to be overwhelmed by feelings and impulses picked up from watching others and acting inappropriately, an inhibitory response is normally activated which limits our reactions. When these inhibitory feedback systems are damaged people do have difficulty distinguishing their own experience from another's.

21 Alexander Broadie is one of the foremost scholars of the Scottish Enlightenment. He summed up this simple 'recipe' for enlightenment in an address to International Futures Forum in November 2001.

22 Though the concept of non-duality crops up in Western philosophy as far back as the Greeks it never really captured the

Western mind before the 20th century. (Loy, 1988). An explosion of interest in Buddhism, Sufism, Taoism, Vedanta, Yoga and other Eastern philosophies in the 1960s brought Eastern concepts of oneness, non-dualism, wu wei to a generation of Western seekers of higher consciousness. See, for example, Walter T. Anderson (1979) and Alan Watts (1961) for influential early explorations of the limitations of egocentric consciousness for the lay person. Coming at wholeness from a more Western direction, the work of physicist David Bohm (1980) also considers Western dualistic thinking that results in a sense of separateness to be an artifact of an ego-bounded consciousness that may be transcended through a process of deep dialogue.

23 Ecclesiastes 3:1

24 Mark Cosgrove, 'The programmer's fear of missing the masterpiece', presentation at Encounter Bristol International Film Festival, November 2011. See http://bit.ly/TPpt17

25 These resources are curated together at www.iffpraxis.com and www.iffacademy.com

Index

adhocracy, 128, 129, 134-136
Albrow, Martin, 136, 137
allophilia, 117
Antonovsky, Aaron, 69, 146,
Ardern, Jacinda, 25, 47
Ariely, Dan, 67, 68, 120

Bateson, Gregory, 38, 182
Bauman, Zygmunt, 96, 118,
   171
Blom, Phillip, 33
Boisot, Max, 135, 136
Broadie, Alexander, 115, 116

Collins, Jim, 26, 142, 180
competence, v, vi, 14-17, 61,
   62, 66, 73, 77, 80, 103
   and culture, 14-17
competencies
   21st-century, 7-9, 14-16,
      19-22, 24, 26-29, 60, 61,
      73, 74, 77, 84-88, 90, 94,
      102, 110, 127, 137, 141-
      146, 151, 155-157, 161-
      167, 169
   core, 63
connoisseurship, 125
Cosgrove, Mark, 125, 126,
   184

Coups, Plenty, 110, 111
creative integrity, 162, 163
Csikszentmihalyi, Mihaly,
   54, 57, 172

defence mechanisms, 58
   denial, 1, 8, 12, 21, 29, 49-
      52, 58, 78
   futility, 58
   jeopardy, 58
   perversity, 58
defensive denial, v, vi, 49-51,
   56
Delors, Jacques, 20, 77, 87,
   141, 168
double task, 21, 22, 78, 86,
   116, 142, 143
Drucker, Peter, 36

Eckersley, Richard, 129
emergencies, three, 8, 12-14,
   36, 41
emergency
   conceptual, 8, 13, 22, 59
Enlightenment, the, vii, 66,
   68, 100, 101, 115, 116, 120,
   122
epistemic awareness, 80
Esalen, 89, 154

185

Festinger, Leon, 49
Frankl, Victor, 71
Freire, Paulo, 54, 148
Freud, Sigmund, 34, 54, 61

Gaia theory, 118
Gawande, Atul, 18
Giffords, Gabrielle, 27
Grimshaw, Alex, 7

Hanna, Thomas, 89
holism, 34
homeschooling, 40

IFF Academy, 156
immigration, 40
individualism, 3, 92, 100,
    109, 182
International Futures Forum,
    4, 9, 24
    IFF Academy, 9
    IFF kitbag, 112, 113, 161-
        164
    IFF Practice Centre, 156,
        159
    IFF prompts, 161

James, William, 84, 88
Jerram, Luke, 112
Jobs, Steve, 47- 49
Jullien, François, 150

Kahane, Adam, 155
Kahneman, Daniel, 67, 72
Kegan, Robert, 54-58, 73
Kitayama, Shinobu, 41

Koestler, Arthur, 70, 104
Konrath, Sara, 102

leadership, 3, 7, 18, 22-27, 36,
    66, 72, 84, 103, 107, 109-
    114, 132, 135, 142, 146,
    149, 159, 170
    cultural leadership, 109–
        11
learning anxiety, 1
learning journeys, 4, 154
learning, four pillars, vi, 87
    being, 88
    being together, 99–102
    learning to do, 127–40
    learning to know, 115–26
Lewin, Kurt, 104, 153
Limits to Growth, 35
literacies, three, 8, 21-23, 78,
    80, 85-87, 113
    cultural literacy, 103–7
Little, Ruth, 93

Marriage, Helen, 133
Maslow, Abraham, 17, 54,
    69-71, 88, 182
May, Rollo, 52
Michael, Don, 13, 35, 36, 90,
    130, 134, 154, 182
Mintzberg, Henry, 128, 129
mirror neurons, 100
MIT Media Lab, 155

nativism, 41
Obama, Barack, 7, 25-28, 40,
    41, 91, 97, 108, 117, 118
Omer, Aftab, 22, 23, 113, 114

organization
  as an integrity, 137
Orlov, Dimitry, 59

Porter, Elsa, 82
practical hope, 9, 165
producer, role of the, 132-
  134, 137, 147, 149
psychosphere, 37–41, 37, 180

qualities of persons of
  tomorrow, 90
  balance, 94
  compassion, 93
  faith in the future, 96–98
  humility, 90–94

Rayner, Steve, 125
rehearsal spaces, 153-157
responses, three, 7, 8, 21, 25,
  47, 49, 52, 56, 59-64, 66,
  70, 78, 84, 92, 96, 131,
  167-170, 183
Rogers, Carl, 11-15, 54, 88,
  97, 104, 154, 179, 182

Schein, Edgar H., v, 1, 5, 7,
  91, 157, 181
Schön, Donald, 85, 134
Seeley Brown, John, 142
Senge, Peter, 145
Sharpe, Bill, 138, 139
Shweder, Richard, 43, 181
Smuts, Jan, 34
Soares, Luiz Eduardo, 112
spiral dynamics, 54
survival anxiety, 1

teamwork, 16, 131
transformative innovation, 9,
  142
Trump, Donald, 40, 47, 108
trumpet, uncertain, 170

wise groups, 107
World Peace Game, 152

Yankelovich, Daniel, 68

Acknowledgments

This book, like any considered work, has been a long time in the making. It has been informed and energized by one and a half lifetimes' professional experience. And it has been catalysed into production by the past decade and more of our shared experience working in the community that is International Futures Forum. From the very first learning journey to the city of Dundee in 2001, IFF has offered a staggering variety of practical experience and intellectual inquiry in which rich soil this book has grown – as we worked together on community regeneration in Falkirk, for example, on governance and leadership in India, on the future for higher education in the US, on how to respond to the global epidemic of mental illness and mental distress, or how to encourage a healthy creative ecosystem of the arts and culture in the UK. We have learned so much from each and every one of the people we have encountered on these journeys, each in their own way seeking to 'rise to the occasion' in the baffling complexity of the 21st century.

This practical experience has been complemented by deep intellectual inquiry and insight, which in today's world must be both by necessity and choice a social activity. Some of the individuals involved are explicitly referenced and acknowledged in the text: Martin Albrow, Max Boisot, Aftab Omer, Bill Sharpe.

Many others have made equally rich contributions to our evolving understanding in a diverse conversation about 'psychological literacy' that has run for several years: Napier Collyns, Roanne Dods, Len Duhl, Kate Ettinger, Jim Ewing, Margaret Hannah, Pat Heneghan, Tony Hodgson, Bob Horn, Bob Lucas (who also compiled our bibliography), Andrew Lyon, Dick Penny, Noah Raford, Neville Singh, Jennifer Williams (who has also provided the beautiful illustrations). And many more.

Andrew Carey at Triarchy Press has been a meticulous editor, embodying just the right spirit for this kind of book. And a special word of thanks to Eamonn Kelly, another of the early IFF adventurers, whose *Powerful Times* proved the trigger for us to get to work on our own contribution.

About Triarchy Press

Triarchy Press is an independent publisher of books that bring a systemic or contextual approach to many areas of life, including:

Government, Education, Health and other public services ~ Ecology and Regenerative Cultures ~ Leading and Managing Organizations ~ The Money System ~ Psychotherapy and other Expressive Therapies ~ Walking, Psychogeography and Mythogeography ~ Movement and Somatics ~ Innovation ~ The Future and Future Studies

For books by Nora Bateson, Daniel Wahl, Russ Ackoff, Barry Oshry, John Seddon, Phil Smith, Bill Tate, Patricia Lustig, Sandra Reeve, Graham Leicester, Nelisha Wickremasinghe, Bill Sharpe, Alyson Hallett and other remarkable writers, please visit:

www.triarchypress.net

About IFF

International Futures Forum (IFF) is a non-profit organization established to support a transformative response to complex and confounding challenges and to restore the capacity for effective action in today's powerful times.

At the heart of IFF is a deeply informed inter-disciplinary and international network of individuals from a range of backgrounds covering a wide range of diverse perspectives, countries and disciplines. The group meets as a learning community as often as possible, including in plenary session. And it seeks to apply its learning in practice.

IFF takes on complex, seemingly intractable issues – notably in the arenas of health, learning, governance and enterprise – where paradox, ambiguity and complexity characterize the landscape, where rapid change means yesterday's solution no longer works, where long-term needs require a long-term logic and where only genuine innovation has any chance of success.

www.internationalfuturesforum.com ~ **www.iffpraxis.com**

About the Authors

Maureen O'Hara PhD is Professor of Psychology, National University, USA; President Emerita, Saybrook University, San Francisco; and Director, International Futures Forum-US. She is a licensed psychotherapist in practice for over three decades and worked closely with Carl R. Rogers in La Jolla, California - facilitating encounter groups, large group events and training psychotherapists in many countries. Her recent work explores the present and potential future impacts of global cultural shifts on psychological development and emotional wellbeing. Books include *Em busca da vida*, with C.R. Rogers, J.K. Wood and A. Fonseca (Summus,1983); *Ten Things To Do In A Conceptual Emergency*, with G. Leicester (Triarchy, 2009); and the *Handbook of Person-Centered Psychotherapy and Counselling* with M. Cooper, P.Schmid and G. Wyatt (Palgrave Macmillan, 2008). She is married to Robert Lucas with whom she resides in Carlsbad, California, spending as much time as they can with family in Yorkshire and IFF colleagues at the Boathouse, Aberdour.

Graham Leicester is Director of International Futures Forum. IFF's mission is to support a transformative response to the challenges of the times. Graham previously ran Scotland's leading think tank, the Scottish Council Foundation, founded in 1997. From 1984-1995 he served as a diplomat in HM Diplomatic Service, specializing in China (he speaks Mandarin Chinese) and the EU. Between 1995 and 1997 he was senior research fellow with the Constitution Unit at University College London. He has also worked as a freelance professional cellist, including with the BBC Concert Orchestra. He has a strong interest in governance, innovation and education, is a senior adviser to the British Council on those issues, and has previously worked with OECD, the World Bank Institute and other agencies on the themes of governance in a knowledge society and the governance of the long term.

Further support is available through the IFF 'Competence in Complexity' programme based on this book:

iffpraxis.com/competence-in-complexity